Simple Truths

Simple Truths

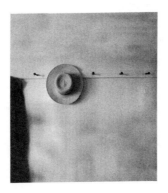

On *Values,* *Civility,*
and Our *Common* *Good*

STEPHEN BAUMAN

Abingdon Press / *Nashville*

SIMPLE TRUTHS

Library of Congress Cataloging-in-Publication Data
Bauman, Stephen.
   Simple truths / Stephen Bauman.
      p. cm.
   ISBN 0-687-33341-5 (binding: printed/casebound : alk. paper)
1. Conduct of life.   2. Truth—Religious aspects—Christianity.   I. Title.

BJ1595.B38 2006
242—dc22

2006003538

06 07 08 09 10 11 12 13 14 15—10 9 8 7 6 5 4 3 2 1
MANUFACTURED IN THE UNITED STATES OF AMERICA

FOR   MELISSA

who teaches the simple truth that love is born
when holding tenderly the weakness of the other.

PREFACE

A number of years ago a friend and spiritual seeker unrelated to my congregation, or, for that matter, my religion, wondered how we might expand our lively two-person conversation pertaining to spirit, meaning, values and our common life. In a few meetings we cooked up the modest plan of buying one-minute segments of radio time and, in effect, giving them away. The idea was to pinprick the brain with a small surprise, something unexpected, a simple truth, that might catch listeners in an off-guard moment and take them down a path they had not intended. My congregation liked the plan.

We chose a robust station that served up only news and information for a big chunk of the eastern seaboard. Well, news, information, and advertisements—plenty of ads—with a rat-a-tat-tat pace that matched the pace of life most people lead today.

As I began preparing these one-minute prompts, I became aware that simple truth is often hidden in plain view. Awash in the tidal force of information intoxication, we're tempted by the proposition that all information bits are equal, nothing is inherently more important, more "true," than anything else. Instinct alone teaches otherwise, but we inevitably succumb to the chaotic undertow of the information tsunami by the simple coincidence of our living in the twenty-first century.

So this collection of transcribed messages implies that certain elemental truths undergird healthy, productive living. For instance, commitment to things like human dignity, integrity, and mature love are essential for vital communities and individual lives redolent with meaning. These are simple truths to which everyone has access.

They are simple truths, even homely in their fashion, but remain buried or ignored, not least because of simple neglect in our clogged environment. This is so even for those who desire greater awareness and a more honest life.

I count myself among those people. As one man—husband, father, friend, citizen, child of God—I want to live with greater attention to the things that up-build my individual life, relationships, and healthy community. Yet, this often seems a lonely enterprise, and I find I am easily distracted. After all, I am making my way in the very same cultural context as everyone else; we share the struggle for identifying and then maintaining the values that promote the common good. And this isn't

easy, even for those who attempt to practice and
advance a particular religious tradition. I know only too
well how religious practice can be overwhelmed by
cultural tidal forces.

Of course, large-scale truth claims compete for our
attention and allegiance, claims of ultimate concern.
Need I say the obvious? These are very important
matters to address. I have heartfelt, passionate beliefs —
made honest by some doubt and ignorance. But
underneath these frameworks, often hidden in the noise
and clatter of routine life and obscured by thoughtless or
selfish action, lie simpler truths that are received like a
cool drink of water from an oasis discovered in a
parched wasteland.

I subscribe to the idea that awareness of simple truth
has its genesis in small moments that accumulate into a
pattern. These patterns lead to decisions and behaviors
that flow into a life with a certain content and direction,
which in turn blend with others whose lives have also
been shaped by simple truth.

There is nothing new here. The mere fact that
something is true reveals its ancient genetics. The small
task I took on was to write and speak to things that
were right in front of us today, fashioning little parables

out of the cloth of our current culture that might tweak our minds to awareness of simple truth, making conscious what had been shrouded by slumber or intoxicants of one form or another.

What follows in these pages then is quite humble. My hope and intent is that they will prompt you to explore the path they suggest, leading to your own more eloquent thinking, exploration, and action. One minute is but a meaningless sound bite—that's one possible response, I suppose. On the other hand, one minute might also be a window on eternity, or at least and more likely, on the next hour.

I think these are best read with space between them. I do not believe you will be especially edified by reading straight through. They are meant to be received one at a time. Let them suggest your own personal work and also the work all of us share. In this sense we'll be in conversation about what matters most. If you want, let me know what you think.

Stephen Bauman
Christ Church
New York City
stephen@stephenbauman.org

ACKNOWLEDGMENTS

This book had its genesis in radio programming prompted through the entrepreneurial spirit of Richard Gilder to whom I extend heartfelt thanks. It would not have developed but for his spontaneous generosity.

This is also the product of the people of Christ Church, United Methodist in New York City, my true home. This wonderful extended family has provided a warm, supportive, and catalytic environment for learning about simple truth (not to mention complex truth).

Special thanks to my colleagues Jonathan Acheson, Richard Allen, Michael Collins, Roseann DeGennaro, Doug Franklin, Cathy Gilliard, Gerry Migliori, Steve Pilkington, and Javier Viera; my friends at WCBS News Radio, Sylvia Herrera and Bill Tynan; John Kutsko of Abingdon Press, Tess Gilder, and Mark Hurst for their various contributions.

Lastly, but importantly, most of what I think I know about simple truth has come by way of learning from my most intimate teachers: Melissa, Luke, Stephanie, Melvin, Adeline, Andy, and Phil. For you, boundless love and gratitude.

I

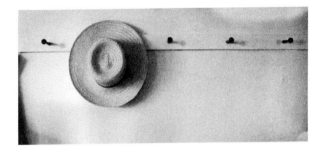

A young woman told me about a spiritual experience that occurred while flipping through TV channels. For a few minutes she was mildly distracted by *Who Wants to Be a Millionaire*, then sailing through something soapy and a talk show concerning the latest trends in cosmetic surgery, she caught a vision of a flood in Africa—people in treetops, arms outstretched to a hovering helicopter. Click. Another channel revealed how the market had fared that day—she was glad the Dow had bounced back a little. Click. Yet another channel brought her the face of a six-year-old girl shot dead at school by a six-year-old boy. Click. Back to *Millionaire* and this question to the contestant, "Was it Billy Joel or John Denver who sang in Russia in 1985?" Then, suddenly, unexpectedly, she said time slowed, the images melded together and she swore she heard a voice say, "Time to wake up!" plain as day. It shook her. Time to wake up—it rang in her ears. It still rang in her ears. Now she said she had no choice. She would have to wake up, whatever that meant, even though she didn't know she had been asleep.

We live in a time when unrestricted, individual expression is thought to be the highest good. We should all be allowed to do whatever we want, whenever we want, wherever we want. So long as that principle is exalted above all others, all other truth is of secondary importance. In this environment, all values are equalized. Every person's truth is equal to every other person's truth. Truth becomes fragmented and personalized, leaving no truth larger than another except, of course, the truth that everyone is free to believe whatever he or she wants. In this world, tolerance ascends the throne as the greatest virtue, which is all well and good until you smack up against something you should not tolerate—physical abuse or racism, for instance. People schooled only in the rights of free expression make for poor citizens in a very complex world of competing claims. Seems to me that our society needs people who look for a truth that's larger than their own self-interest. But in our land, where are these sorts of people nurtured?

While sitting at dinner with boomer friends, the conversation turned to the subject of values education. We commiserated over the paucity of commitment to matters of lasting importance by the public at large. Ann said that from her experience struggling through a business start-up, she had learned how important it was to have drive to accomplish anything of significance. Drive was the value ticket to success. In the silent digestion that followed, I remembered a time my father told me that very thing. I'm sure it came on a day I was lazed in front of the tube that he said, "Steve, what you need in life is drive . . . won't amount to anything without it!" He then gave me a paragraph written by a motivational speaker that I still have stashed away in an old shoe box. Somewhere along the line I came to agree that drive was a fine, even necessary, quality for a life that had a competent outcome. Still, it remains a lesser virtue. Our most important values concern the goal of our driving. Seems to me that an evil person with drive causes a whole lot more damage than one who's lazy.

Returning home from church one Sunday, President Abraham Lincoln was asked by a companion how he liked the sermon. Mr. Lincoln responded that he thought the message was well prepared and thoughtfully constructed but that it lacked the most important ingredient. His companion asked what that was. The president responded, "The preacher failed to ask us to do anything great." When was the last time you were invited to do something great, something that required sacrificial behavior on your part that led to your own character development while also accomplishing some good? There is precious little conversation about this sort of thing in our culture. More often, we are likely to hear the advice that invites us to take the ethical shortcut, the easiest route that asks the least of us, focused on very short-term goals. What would happen if we developed the habit of encouraging one another to take the more difficult path, in effect, to do something great, something that dignified our humanity rather than simply exploited it?

Among the popular New Year's resolutions that are proffered every January by well-meaning persons are those pertaining to work. These run the gamut from desiring a different job, spending more time at home, or being more competent. Although these intentions most often are rarely implemented, they do point to a very important series of considerations. Fact is, how we work in the world has a profound impact on the quality and content of every other aspect of our lives. Frederick Douglass said that "a man is worked upon by what he works on. He may carve out his circumstances, but his circumstances will carve him out as well." That's consistent with what I see in people, and it suggests that we ought to care a lot about how we pay out our lives. Whatever we spend our time and energy on in the world is what will end up shaping us. For instance, we can't have peace and happiness if we spend the greater portion of our lives clawing and scraping for dominance and power. Stands to reason, you become what you prize.

We don't hear much about the virtue of fidelity these days. Can't remember the last time I heard that word pass the lips of any commentator or politician. The Marines, whose motto, *Semper Fidelis,* meaning "always faithful," still invest themselves in its military applications, but I can't think of any school, work, or media environment to which I've been exposed where fidelity receives the slightest mention. Cicero said long ago that "nothing is more noble, nothing more venerable than fidelity. Faithfulness and truth are the most sacred excellences and endowments of the human mind." Sounds out of step with our current context, though, doesn't it? Old-fashioned. And yet, it's hard to imagine a life of deep meaning that doesn't have at its core a commitment to the truth. What do you think: if you had to choose, would you rather be famous, wealthy, powerful, or faithful?

Do you highly value your time? Planning consultant and CEO of Search Technology William Rouse reports how it never ceases to amaze him "how much time people say they spend doing things they claim not to value. At the same time, they emphasize how little time they spend doing things they profess to value. People often tend to reflect wistfully on all the things they wish they were doing. However, they do not act. In this way, they squander their time. They are wasting their most precious resource." Dear reader, how about a truthful response: Is that you? Do you ever find yourself whining how little time you have to spend on things you say matter most? Experience reveals that we are great pretenders. If something *really does* matter to us, we make the time for it. Check it out in your own life. If you're serious about changing your habits, keep a time journal for a month. Take stock. And then, for your own soul's sake, act. You have exactly one lifetime. It would be a horrible waste to let it dribble away.

I heard an interesting statistic as I channel-surfed the morning news programs: sixty-five million dollars are spent each day in the United States on books and seventy-eight million dollars are spent on lotteries. What's particularly ironic about these figures is that most states designate their earnings from lotteries to education. We all know by now that lotteries take the most from persons least able to afford them, so the effect is like a substantial tax bite on families who could use the extra cash for things, such as books for the kids. Now I have bought a ticket or two when the payout has sailed past ten million dollars, but I have no illusions that by doing so I've advanced the cause of education or social policy. When one considers that chances are far better to be struck by lightning than to hit the jackpot, logic dictates five or ten dollars could be put to much better use. Here's a better bet for the new year: once a week, once a month, or just once in a while, buy a book for someone you love.

I am completely up-to-date in the communications department. I have several e-mail addresses, high-speed Internet access, calling card, cell phone/PDA, desktop and portable computers, plenty of televisions, six wireless/two-line, extension phones in my home — you name it. Since many are commuting when they hear my radio spots, occasionally I'll receive a phone call from the car, bus, or train to offer commentary, which underscores how we're hooked up like never before. But the other day my daughter phoned from college with a pressing problem. I hit the call-waiting flash, told her I was on another call but said I'd get right back to her, while scrolling through e-mail. I returned to my original call, completed business, and became captured by the messages in my inbox. A full twelve hours lapsed before I remembered she had telephoned. When it came to me, I sat quietly for a moment musing on how reachable we are, how available — and yet how prone we remain to missing authentic connection.

A catalogue of the Learning Annex advertised a remarkably eclectic assortment of classes and workshops, claiming they would help you take charge of your future. From instruction on how to master the Worldwide Web, to the fine art of erotic photography, there were offerings for just about every want, need, and taste. But, if you really, really wanted a permanent new you, a course was advertised as "How to Change Your Identity." It dealt with topics such as how to plan your disappearance; how to obtain a new birth certificate; how to transform your physical appearance; how to concoct a reasonable "history" for your new persona; and so on. Based on my experience with people, I'm guessing that was a popular course. So many say they'd like a fresh take on their lives. Here's a very small suggestion if you're among them: before you completely check out of the old "you," check into a religious establishment. Though not nearly as dramatic a solution, you might find the key to seeing your true identity when you look in a mirror.

I heard a story about a man from Philadelphia. He murdered a driver who had slipped in front of his car on a congested expressway. Evidently the delay was caused by several lanes merging into one, and he had been waiting, stewing in frustration for a long time. Just as his turn came to move into the funnel neck, another guy, driving the shoulder, squeezed past, laughed, and gestured with a certain finger. The scorned driver blew a gasket. Later on, having followed his antagonist, he saw his chance at revenge when once again traffic came to a stop. He pulled a gun out of his glove compartment, got out of his car, walked over to the window of the offending driver, and shot him dead. Now, truth be told, there's more than one reader who has fantasized something similar a time or two; fortunately, we usually have the good sense not to confuse fantasy with reality. But even so, consider the damage we do through simple, narcissistic, emotional self-indulgence in the course of just one day. If you pay attention, you're bound to witness a murder or two—or even commit one.

More than ever before we live in a time of competing religious truths. I'm passionate about mine, as most readers are about theirs. That's healthy and makes for a robust society, that is, so long as there's a shared value of respect. A great teacher once said: "Believe nothing merely because you have been told it, or because it is traditional, or because you yourselves have imagined it. Do not believe what your teacher tells you merely out of respect. But whatsoever you find to be conducive to the good, the benefit of all beings—that doctrine believe and cling to, and take it as your guide." My own faith—which I hold is of universal import—is not diminished by these truthful words even though they were spoken by the Buddha. I find them consistent with what I believe. My faith practice is strongest when it embraces truth in all the forms it appears. After all, in telling others about my deepest truths, I'm hoping for a respectful reception. And in any case, as the years wear on, the *biggest* truth will have its way eventually, regardless of whatever any of us say today.

II

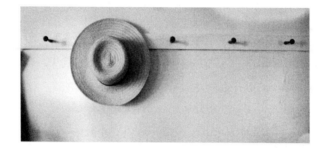

The middle-aged man in my office was reporting a lifetime series of failed relationships with his several wives, children, and business partners. He had lived life to the fullest, he said, and though he should probably feel more guilt than he did, he wasn't entirely displeased with what he had experienced. Interesting experience, after all, is what gave zest to his life. He loved the freedom to do whatever he pleased, whenever he pleased. He was a true libertarian, he claimed. I asked what brought him to my door, then. With that he fell silent and eventually offered that he had this growing, gnawing emptiness inside. He wanted a relationship with his children who despised him. He knew he needed help, but he didn't want to give up his freewheeling ways. Historian Gertrude Himmelfarb tweaked an old saying this way: "Absolute liberty may also corrupt absolutely." Freedom without responsible commitments has no meaning. That's a simple truth that takes many a lifetime to learn.

There's a common complaint I hear from a wide array of people. They may state this complaint in different ways, and experience it somewhat differently, but it boils down to this: their lives are out of balance. They have some of one thing, but not nearly enough of another. They feel off kilter, lopsided, both overfull and strangely empty. Rumer Godden has written of an Indian proverb or axiom that says that "everyone is a house with four rooms, a physical, a mental, an emotional, and a spiritual. Most of us tend to live in one room most of the time but, unless we go into every room every day, even if only to keep it aired, we are not a complete person." I think failing to routinely visit each of these rooms is often behind our feeling of disorientation. We are strangely unaware that simple disciplines of attention to these various conditions can restore the experience of balance and well-being to a remarkable degree. Write those four words on a slip of paper and place it where you will see it each day as a reminder. You'll be surprised how soon they become second nature and hard to forget.

Having arrived at a certain age, I've been talking pension plans with a financial planner who presses me to consider the sort of retirement I want, and when I want it. I'm finding this a difficult exercise. I know the fastest growing age group on a percentage basis is centenarians. That means that, quite possibly, half my life remains to be lived. It's hard to plan that far ahead. But I know I do want these next decades to be richly meaningful. I don't want to check out too early. Philosopher Søren Kierkegaard once said that a student allotted four hours on a written test gained nothing by finishing early. In fact, he said, "It becomes a fault to finish before the time has transpired. Suppose a man were given the task of entertaining himself for an entire day, and he finishes this task of self-entertainment as early as noon: then his celerity would not be meritorious. So also when life constitutes the task. To be finished with life before life has finished with one, is precisely not to have finished the task." Perhaps, in addition to actuarial tables, investment terminology, and health-care advice, retirement handbooks should contain this reminder.

I'm intrigued by the number of people I speak with who complain about their disappointment with romance. If that sounds like you, you're in very good company. You are certainly not alone, even though you may feel like just about the loneliest person in the world. I'm equally intrigued with a recurring theme in the stories many people tell. I can't recount how many times an individual has told me he or she has a propensity to fall in love with the very sort of person who is a most ill-suited match for a long-term relationship. There are a variety of ways to get at this psychologically, no two exactly alike, but a general rule persists: if you experience a paradoxical behavior pattern, you have a window into something that is profoundly truthful about yourself, and you are presented with a great opportunity for deepening your own self-awareness. Seemingly mature adults still have a lot of growing up to do, but once the adolescent threshold has been breached, this growing up becomes a matter of choice. The trick is to actually do the choosing.

Waiting at a bus stop, I realized a new community has been forming for some time now just below the radar. A community that is bound by shared need. It's the community of dispossessed smokers in a city that has made the habit illegal in nearly every public environment. No longer tolerated by their peers and now huddled in the entryway of their office tower, stood an odd mix of persons representing a broad spectrum of city dwellers. Old and young, seemingly rich and not-so-rich, black and white and Asian, an executive in a three-piece suit standing with a latex-clad messenger, women from well coiffed to grunge, sharing a spirited and light-hearted conversation while intermittently puffing, laughing, coughing, and shivering. It was actually quite impressive in its own way. It made me long for a more robust sort of city-wide community, a community bound up by far larger causes than nicotine addiction. A community that was equally unconcerned with race, ethnicity, and appearance in addressing a common need. Ironic how these "dispossessed" revealed a deeper truth.

Quite a number of years ago I was involved in a musical comedy production at my children's school. I played the male romantic lead, which required me to kiss the ingénue. This prompted an interesting conversation with my kids, who were then six and eight years old. More than once they witnessed me practicing this moment of dramatic intimacy. They were both embarrassed and very curious about our relationship. One night around the dinner table I was asked if I liked kissing this other woman. I shrewdly responded by saying that we were simply pretending to be in love. Real love, I said, was all about living out commitments, being responsible to one another, helping each other, just like how we did at home. Anything that happened on stage was left there and had no meaning beyond the story. At home, we built a life based on our relationships. My son piped up and said, "Well, Dad, it sure looked real." "Just great acting," my wife replied as I took my dishes out to the kitchen.

I sat at a crowded luncheon counter enjoying a grilled cheese and tomato sandwich when two guys, who I guessed were in their mid- to late-twenties, squeezed into the seats next to me. I quickly surmised they had both been recently laid off from work, and if I were to have judged the fate of humanity on the basis of their bleak outlook, I would have suggested we all have a drink and call it a day. Man, were they down on their lives! At one point one of them said he had no hope. So young with no hope. I don't know the precise key to move from hopelessness to hopefulness, but I believe a choice is often involved. Martin Luther King Jr. once said, "I am personally the victim of deferred dreams, of blasted hopes, but in spite of that I close today by saying I still have a dream, because, you know, you can't give up in life. If you lose hope, somehow you lose that vitality that keeps life moving, you lose that courage to be, that quality that helps you go on in spite of all. And so today I still have a dream." I wished I could have said something like that to those guys. The best I could do was to write it up as a reminder for some other anonymous person.

February is presidents' month. We even have a day off to help us remember this. Given our national preoccupation with our security and place in the world, consideration of our national heroes is in order. For me, Abraham Lincoln towers above most others, and an examination of his agonies of statecraft seem particularly relevant whenever our nation must act out of its most cherished values. Many scholars believe Lincoln was a better thinker on moral-political issues than all of the theologians and philosophers of his day. Interestingly, he was never a member of any church, though a reasonably regular attendee. There's no better primer on the moral underpinnings of political action than a good biography of Lincoln. We would do ourselves, as well as our nation, a good service by picking one up and considering the responsibilities of moral, political virtue. These days require the best from the American people. We need to sit at the feet of our greatest.

An article in the *Financial Times* announced that belief in consumer brands has replaced religious faith as the thing that gives purpose to people's lives. "Brands are the new religion. People turn to them for meaning," declared the advertising firm of Young and Rubicam. Fitch, the London design consultancy, reported that many people flocked to IKEA instead of church on Sundays. Since 1991, Fitch continued, twelve thousand people have been married at Disney World, and it is now common for Harley-Davidson motorcycle aficionados to be buried in Harley-branded coffins. Young and Rubicam claimed that today's brand builders could be compared to the missionaries of former times; they stand not just for quality but for a set of beliefs. Or should I say "briefs" since Calvin Klein was one named exemplar of the new "belief brands." Now, I've always known that we humans can't escape living our lives without believing in something. But I didn't think it was Coca-Cola, Nike, and BMW.

Squeezing into the last available banquette in a crowded diner I sat very near to a thirty-something woman chattering away on her cell phone. As soon as I heard the words "boyfriend," "sex," and "Hamptons," I knew I was in the wrong seat. Ordering my lunch, I was accompanied by her description of commitment in the early days of the twenty-first century—and it was mighty thin gruel. Ranging through the details of a relationship with someone named Alec—poor Alec—I learned he was the last in a long line of guys with whom she "fooled with." Still, for a brief moment I found myself a little wistful about the romantic idea of a life unencumbered by commitment. That was the person she revealed: completely consumed with self. I heard only about a woman on the take, which snapped my attention to the fact I couldn't think of anything truly worthwhile in my life that was not the result of mundane commitment. I thought of that later at dinner, sharing the events of the day with my wonderful daughter.

Walking to work one morning, I found my
attention captured by loud voices. Turning in
the direction of the source, I saw a young African
American female cop yelling at a white middle-aged
driver. Intrigued, I moved closer. I observed an enraged
police officer attempting to correct the behavior and the
attitude of the driver. What became immediately
apparent was that the driver had zero respect for the
officer. And this lack of respect had to do with her
gender if not her race. This was an instant gut
assessment on my part, but I'm sure I was right—I
recognized the patterned instincts. I knew in an instant
that had this driver been dealing with a middle-aged
white male cop, the exchange would have been entirely
different. Later that morning I read a story in the *Wall
Street Journal* that concerned the significant gender and
race gap in congressional elections across the nation ...

The *New York Times* reported that physicists are completely stumped over a new problem. Apparently empty space isn't quite as empty as they once thought. Numerous independent observations indicate that a mysterious force pushes against gravity causing the universe to expand at an accelerating pace. It defies conventional logic, but this leads scientists to try to answer this question: how much does emptiness weigh? No one can yet answer this question, but I take some comfort knowing that unanswerable questions exist elsewhere in our land. Questions like, following one of the longest running economic booms in our history, why are some city schools still warmed by coal and why are the homeless and mentally ill left to wander the streets? What is the mysterious force that causes the gap between rich and poor to expand at an accelerating pace? I know that considerable brain power will be devoted to answering science's questions. I wonder how much will be brought to bear on these other tough questions.

A short time ago we moved from a Manhattan rental apartment to a condominium. Setting aside the fact these new digs were purchased at the tippy-top of the market and renovations proved the maxim about construction delays leaving us to live amidst plaster dust, open walls, and stacked boxes, I can happily report we did the right thing and that I feel fortunate to be occupying the new place. Very fortunate. I even imagined this change would open a new chapter in my own life. Of course, twelve-step programs speak of the dangers of the "geographical cure," cautioning that, as the title of a popular book put it a number of years ago, "wherever you go, there you are." The important reminder here: authentic change takes place *within* a person, not in his or her external surroundings. If a bright new chapter were to unfold for me, it would come because I made it so from the inside out, not because I was distracted by the pleasure and pain of going condo. I find it helpful to write this down here, so by my sharing, you can help me own my best intentions.

I invite you to check out a remarkable and important exhibition online entitled, *Without Sanctuary: Photographs and Postcards of Lynching in America*. Type that into your search engine and you will be able to find this challenging educational collection. I first came in contact with these photographs at the New York Historical Society. I was unprepared for what I witnessed at the exhibit. The walls of the display room were lined with small photographs of American lynchings between 1890 and 1930. The victims were mostly black. Many of the pictures were souvenir postcards that had been printed by the hundreds and sent around the nation. Here's a warning: this is a very disturbing, yet simultaneously profoundly compelling experience. Why didn't I know that *thousands* of such lynchings took place within those few decades, with *thousands* of people—including many children who had been let out of school to witness the spectacles—captured for all time, often in jacket and tie, gathered around a body hanging in a very public place? Why has there been such collective amnesia surrounding this truth? That question haunts me.

III

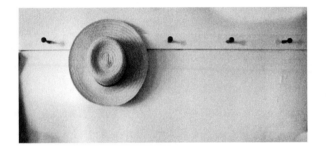

The science section of the *New York Times* ran a front-page story concerning evil. It seems that for some forensic scientists, no other word better captures certain diagnoses of human behavior. Psychiatrists at New York and Columbia universities are encouraging their profession not to shrink from thinking in terms of evil when appraising certain offenders. I'm inclined to agree. However, those of us who regularly consider spiritual concerns know this matter of evil and so-called "evil-doers" is more complex than it first appears. Nobel prize-winning author Aleksandr I. Solzhenitsyn, a victim of torture in the Soviet Gulag, reflected, "If only there were evil people somewhere insidiously committing evil deeds, and it were necessary only to separate them from the rest of us and destroy them. But the line dividing good and evil cuts through the heart of every human being. And who is willing to destroy a piece of his own heart?" Hard as they might try, psychiatrists can never answer that question. That conundrum dwells with each one of us and requires us to perform a type of heart surgery on ourselves.

The out-of-place, odd-sounding name, "Columbine High School," has been burned into our collective memory forever, pricking our conscience every time we hear it. The night of the massacre, I watched the special news report with my teenaged son, which made the story all the more chilling. The seemingly random location and boy-next-door quality to the killers' appearances added to a sense of threat at close proximity. At the report's conclusion, and after a moment of silence, my son blurted out, "You know, Dad, the suburbs are really wack!" As a New Yorker, the statement had more than a little irony given the national impression of life on the mean urban streets. From his vantage point, however, he believed the danger was somewhere other than where he was. Yet surely one of the truer lessons of this awful episode was that no one has the luxury of believing the darker forces of our culture are located somewhere else and are someone else's problem. Vigilance for our common good belongs to everyone.

In a recent conversation with a young man preparing for college, he asked me if I thought he was foolish for not taking advantage of a recent opportunity to cheat on the SAT. He said the proctor was very encouraging of the students to take more time than officially allotted to be sure they had done all they could on each of the sections. "Go ahead, help each other out." The majority availed themselves of the proctor's offer. However, he had stuck with the formal time restraints and was now wondering if that was foolish given the cutthroat competition of the college process. On a very basic level he was asking me whether success or integrity was more important. I was impressed he was questioning this at all because the current cultural climate is so heavily weighted on the side of success-at-all-costs. Was he a fool? Well, I said in a sense he was, but I added, it was just this sort of foolishness that helped the human race grow into its greatest glory. If only we had more fools just like him.

The *Wall Street Journal* reported that the demographics among younger singles have shifted. In the perennial search for a mate, not so long ago the numbers favored men. Times have changed, especially for men aged thirty to forty-four. And even more so for those men who seek a somewhat younger mate. By the year 2010, single men in their late thirties and early forties will outnumber women five to ten years younger by two to one. This turnabout has an obvious good news/bad news aspect. Good news for women, bad news for men. Matchmakers and dating companies are already seeing the impact. One reports the male membership has soared twenty-five-fold since it began just a short number of years ago. The myth of the desperate single woman seems on the wane. Guys, here's a tip: you're going to be needing something a bit more compelling than certain basic anatomical features and biological abilities—like a life, for instance, that's worth sharing.

I read in a newspaper about a study on human competency. Perhaps not surprisingly, researchers discovered that persons who are in some manner or form deemed incompetent by a reasonable standard do not believe that they are. They rate themselves as quite capable. In other words, incompetent people don't know that they're incompetent and probably won't believe it if you tell them. That's one of the marks of incompetence. Bad news for bosses everywhere, assuming, of course, the bosses are competent. All of us have our relative strengths and weaknesses, of course. The trick to living in the real world is to be objective about this. The people I have admired the most over the years are constant learners. They have not believed they had it all or knew it all. Some have had quite a lot of power, some have not. What they have all shared, however, was an ability to see what was true, especially what was true about themselves. Alas, the article got me thinking about everyone else I know.

In stories concerning the egregious treason of FBI agent Robert Hanssen, news sources reported that he was a classic churchgoing Dad, driving an old Volkswagen van. People described him as a helpful neighbor with a wife and six typical kids. I recall one neighbor's comment that "They went to church every Sunday—if that means anything." The phrase, "if that means anything," caught my attention. No one could have known the interior of his mind, of course. We have a hard enough time knowing our own, which is the intriguing lesson for anyone with the stomach to look at the status of their own commitments. I can imagine that Richard Nixon meant it when he said in his 1968 nomination acceptance speech, "Let us begin by committing ourselves to the truth, to see it like it is and tell it like it is, to tell the truth, to speak the truth and to live the truth. That's what we will do." He might have meant that in the moment. Then again he might quite knowingly have hid behind those words, wearing them as a sort of "deep cover." That's what came up for me in the Hanssen story. I wondered if I could be accused of living a "deep cover" sort of life. After all, what better role than minister.

A number of years ago my family and I took a whirlwind tour of three European cities, including Rome. On a whim prior to leaving, I checked in with several Catholic friends to see if we might attend something at Saint Peter's Basilica at which the pope was in attendance. Far exceeding my expectations, when we arrived at our hotel, tickets had arrived that put us in the front row of the next day's papal audience in Saint Peter's Square. And I confess that this Methodist family was more than impressed by the spectacle, pomp, and power of the event. Each of us greeting John Paul II and receiving his blessing was a high point of our trip. Now there's much in the details of policy and theology about which I did not agree with this pope. However, I found his courage and fortitude compelling, even inspiring, and the church over which he presided impressive in substance and tradition. I'm grateful for the historic faith we share and long for the day when the spirit of unity will gain precedence over that which divides and separates, spilling outward to people of other faiths entirely.

The Music Educators National Conference compiled a list of forty-two songs that it says Americans "must continue singing . . . to preserve an important part of the national culture." Among the suggested tunes are: "I've Been Workin' on the Railroad," "Oh! Susanna," and "Amazing Grace," which made me wonder if they understood the latter was a religious song, notwithstanding many modern renditions. The legend of the hymn goes that John Newton was transporting slaves when a storm hit his boat. He was converted on the spot, released the slaves, returned to England, and wrote the song. That's the sentimental version. Actually, Newton didn't change his mind about slavery until many years after his conversion, which, I must confess, I hear as a cautionary tale for my own life and presumptions. I applaud the Music Educators' suggestions. I hope they recommend the whole story be told as the music is taught. After all, this lagging moral maturation is as much a part of our national culture as our music.

Several years ago the Beatles' lead guitarist, George Harrison, succumbed to a long battle with cancer. The day the story broke, it led most news reports to address the profound impact this legendary group had on popular culture. The Beatles led the charge in the rebellious sixties—often reviled by parents as they were idolized by youth. The youth then, of course, are now the middle-aged and older, although, as for that, the Beatles' music has held up extremely well and has been embraced by successive generations. Interestingly, the obituary I read at the time included an oft-repeated comment made by Harrison who said, "Everything else can wait, but the search for God cannot wait." Ahead of his time forty-some years ago, I wonder if he wasn't right on time for today. Perhaps it was his prolonged confrontation with mortality that catalyzed this homely wisdom. Given his notoriety I thought this quiet expression served to amplify the wake-up call we've experienced in these first years of the new millennium.

Mark was standing in my office, hands on hips, occasionally raising a hand to stab the air with his index finger. An alcoholic in denial, Mark was explaining to me why he didn't need anybody's help to get his life in order. He didn't need a therapist, he didn't need AA, and he most assuredly didn't need a minister. His family and career in shambles, Mark was adamant he would go it alone. Here's a parable for our time as told by Rabbi David Wolpe. "A boy and his father were walking along a road when they came across a large stone. The boy said to his father, 'Do you think if I use all my strength, I can move this rock?' His father answered, 'If you use all your strength, I am sure you can do it.' The boy began to push the rock. Exerting himself as much as he could, he pushed and pushed. The rock did not move. Discouraged, he said to his father, 'You were wrong, I can't do it.' His father placed his arm around the boy's shoulder and said, 'No son, you didn't use all your strength—you didn't ask me to help.'" Get it, Mark? Leaning on others is both a necessity and a good example. We need it especially at certain times . . . or is it all the time?

My friend had been beaten down by several tragedies. Her daughter had drowned in the backyard pool while celebrating her third birthday with friends. During the subsequent counseling, her husband fell in love with the therapist whose professional boundaries were exceeded by passion. Divorce ensued. Two years later I sat with this same friend whose other daughter now lay in a coma following an accident. She told me she had lost all hope. And she asked where she might find some. She was not optimistic about her future. At that moment I didn't have the words, but I did take her hand. Later that day I stumbled on this wisdom from Václav Havel, who said, "[Hope] transcends the world that is immediately experienced, and is anchored somewhere beyond its horizons . . . Hope is definitely not the same thing as optimism." Those of us in the religion business dare to name and describe that source of hope. We use different words and images, but all point to something larger than ourselves because we instinctively know that hope can't really be hope, unless its capacity outstrips our own puny powers.

A friend walked onto the subway train and sat down in the last available seat. Several stops later a large, late-term pregnant woman lumbered on board and my friend rose to offer his seat, which she gladly accepted. Except, she was a tad broader in the beam than the seat that evidently had been designed for a skinny eight-year-old. Well, this triggered a domino effect of sliding, squeezing, and scrunching down the row of seats until the ripple hit a large man in a business suit who had no intention of moving anywhere for anyone. This annoyed the hell out of the man who slid into him. Words were exchanged. They both stood up. Fists at the ready, the train lurched as the brakeman made a hard stop. The businessman lost his footing, banged his head on a center bar, and landed on his knees as his opponent reseated himself in the only remaining seat. Without missing a beat, my friend then politely thanked the man for standing so the pregnant woman could sit. A study in civility, New York City style.

In the once notorious novel, *The Catcher in the Rye*, Holden Caulfield speaks about his problem with praying: "If you want to know the truth," he says, "I can't even stand ministers. The ones they've had at every school I've gone to, they all have these Holy Joe voices when they start giving their sermons. God, I hate that. I don't see why the hell they can't talk in their natural voice. They sound so phony when they talk." Unknowingly, Holden is addressing the issue of integrity here. Re-reading this classic that was assigned to my son, I've decided to keep his words close; I want to be reminded about the difference between acting, or playing, a role and living authentically. Ministers are sitting ducks for the accusation, "practice what you preach," much the way doctors are for "physician, heal thyself." But the truth is, everyone has this integrity issue in one form or another. It comes right along with the assignments of spouse, parent, employee, boss, citizen, friend, or most simply, person. Integrity is the character trait that stands behind all others. Holden instinctively understood that.

It happened on the Long Island Railroad. During his morning commute, a friend watched as two men, three rows ahead, worked themselves into an agitated argument. One was a burly Paul Bunyan type, the other was slight and spoke only limited English. As the scene unfolded, the larger man reached for something on the rack above that he then swiftly banged on the head of the smaller man who yelped in pain. My friend watched in wonderment as he realized the weapon of choice was a copy of *The Seven Habits of Highly Effective People,* Stephen R. Covey's paean to personal mastery. I guess even highly effective people lose their composure sometimes. Or maybe the anonymous commuter hadn't yet reached the stage of "personal effectiveness." Grabbing my old copy off the shelf, I find that the first habit Covey espouses is: be proactive. Evidently the book-wielding man either misunderstood or had not yet read the line that says, "If I really want to improve my situation, I can work on the one thing over which I have control — myself."

IV

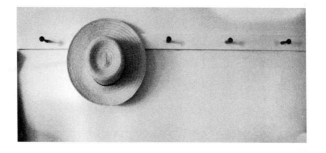

Risking his life to film the systematic murder of his
fellow countrymen, journalist Sorious Samura of
Sierra Leone described in a CNN program a nation in
dire need, a nation that was being murdered, a country
that was dying, that was being left to die by the Western
world, by the so-called developed world. "Kill every
living thing," demanded the rebel forces as they entered
Freetown, his nation's capital, in January of 1999.
Samura told a powerful, award-winning story about
greed, corruption, and brutality. It was a story that
revealed the sometimes paper-thin reality of human
civilization. The horrific massacre in Sierra Leone was
an extreme example of the collapse of common decency,
but I have been brooding on the fact that hard-won
concepts of enlightened civilization can be destroyed by
explosive brutality as well as by slow-eating corrosion.
Both the hot furnace and rust can consume iron. One
just takes a lot longer. I've been wondering about
examples of this slower variety.

The young woman was expressing her grave anxiety over the state of the world. The ongoing war, continuing acts of terrorism, the state of health care. She was an optimist by nature, she said, but lately she was waking in the middle of the night with fevered dreams. She wondered if I agreed with the Dalai Lama who reflected, "I am convinced that human nature is basically gentle, not aggressive. And every one of us has a responsibility to act as if all our thoughts, words, and deeds matter: For, really, they do. Our lives have both purpose and meaning." I told my young friend I very much agreed with that last sentiment, but that I was less sure of the first. I was not at all certain we humans were gentle by nature; experience suggested otherwise, which was all the more reason why our thoughts, words, and deeds did matter. She concurred. I suggested she might want to find a community of persons who shared that conviction. I bet it would help her sleep better.

A certain billionaire's ex-wife asked the state court for $320,000 a month to care for their three-year-old daughter, the biggest child-support request ever in California. Married for just one month, the Mrs. stipulated that her little one needed $14,000 a month for parties, $5,900 for eating out, a measly $4,300 for eating in. Then there was the $436 a month required to care for a bunny and other pets, which, I noted at the time, was more than my son's room at college. Oh, and of course, the $144,000 needed for travel on private jets. Evidently being a three-year-old these days isn't what it used to be, with all the jetting, partying, and pet maintenance required. You've got to hand it to Mom, though. She clearly understood how to soften the blow of a devastating divorce.

I went to bed irritated last night and I woke up with the same irritation. I won't bore you with the details, but suffice it to say this irritation is chronic and unavoidable. I'm not certain what to do about the cause, and I don't like the helplessness this engenders. Call it serendipity: before I headed out the door this morning, I glanced at an open book on the counter and happened to read this quote that was attributed to Harry Emerson Fosdick, a renowned preacher of the first half of the last century. "The most extraordinary thing about the oyster is this. Irritations get into his shell. He does not like them. But when he cannot get rid of them, he uses the irritation to do the loveliest thing an oyster ever has a chance to do. If there are irritations in our lives today, there is only one prescription: make a pearl. It may have to be a pearl of patience, but, anyhow, make a pearl. And it takes faith and love to do it." Initially, the seeming sentimentality of this bit of wisdom irritated me too. But as the day wore on, I found that by letting go of my attachment to irritation, I was on my way to creating, if not a pearl, a much healthier frame of mind.

Standing on the subway platform, I could feel the blood-red anxiety rise in my system. It was the fight or flight response, an adrenaline rush that felt hostile. I had been waiting for only ten minutes but the crowd had grown to claustrophobic proportions, and I had counted seven trains traveling in the opposite direction. Where was mine? When I became aware of sputtering and muttering under my breath, I realized how foolish I was to get this worked up over something for which I had absolutely no control. I glanced around and saw that I was not alone in my soliloquies to stress. Actually, it was rather amusing to witness the numbers of persons strutting and muttering, somehow convinced they had been singled out for this punishment. What a waste to give in to it! As soon as I had this thought, the anxiety retreated, and I knew I would arrive at my destination with a far more appropriate disposition. My family would be glad for that. Another gentle reminder that serenity is there every time I remember I am not the center of the universe.

My wife and I recently took a stroll through the new Bed Bath & Beyond in our neighborhood, the huge emporium dedicated to satisfying every household need. We thought we'd just look around, but the hunger began the moment we walked through the doors. Honey, look at those neat corkscrews. And over there, those nifty thermos cups. Further in we found buckets and brooms, spice racks and vacuum cleaners, and a new deluxe George Foreman grill. Did we need help? Could we use a shopping cart? No thank you. But that was before walking into linens, where we realized we could use some new sheets, and come to think of it, how about that comforter? Might as well upgrade our pillows. Neat coffeemaker. The dish towels match the kitchen floor. What a plunger! We need that. Should get a new mop too. And for dessert: mugs, picture frames, and pop-up laundry hampers. What a feast. Or was it? It's hard to watch your diet when there's just so much good stuff to consume. But isn't a diet generally a good thing?

There's a great group of people at my church. We're not a really large congregation, but we reflect the rich variety of New York City. We have people from all around town, all the boroughs, Westchester County, and New Jersey—represented are at least forty national and ethnic identities. Increasingly, I appreciate how they wish to anchor their budding faith in tangible acts. They continually push me to expand the range of my own compassion. This is a good thing. Rabbi David Wolpe tells the story of a man standing before God, his heart breaking from the pain and injustice in the world. "'Dear God,' he cried out, 'look at all the suffering and distress in Your world. Why don't you send help?' God responded, 'I did send help. I sent you.'" Interestingly, that's from a book entitled *Teaching Your Children About God*. Like many lessons we reserve for children, I find this one especially poignant for adults. Thankfully, there are centers where this sort of adult learning takes place—learning that has the power to change the world. Why not check one out in your town.

What do you believe in? What is the essential commitment of your life? Most religious traditions concern themselves with questions like this. Of course, it's entirely possible to loosely associate with some faith tradition and miss the real point of it. An old joke puts it this way: A six-year-old came home from school one day upset over a conversation she had with one of her friends. The friend informed her that she didn't believe in God. For one whose earliest memories revolved around church, this came as quite a shock. After discussing the matter with her mother in great detail, she thought for a while, then said to her mother: "Well, I guess if they don't believe in God, they don't go to brunch." It's certainly possible to subscribe to some pious ideas that are rather pleasant, affirming, and unchallenging but subsequently completely irrelevant to the living of our days. Underneath everything that occupies your time, what could you say was your *essential* commitment? Do you have one? Do you need one? Or is brunch quite adequate, thank you!

In response to rampant crime and corruption problems in the last decade, the Religious Leaders Forum of South Africa organized a national "Morals Summit." That nation's political and religious leadership gathered to discuss the spiritual and moral malaise besetting South Africa. "Our nation is experiencing a deep moral crisis," the religious leaders declared. "Widespread cooperation of its people and institutions is necessary to bring about a realistic transformation." Then-President Nelson Mandela added, "Social transformation of our country cannot be separated from its spiritual transformation." The Summit called on everyone in positions of authority to sign a code of conduct incorporating ten principles: integrity, incorruptibility, good faith, impartiality, openness, accountability, justice, respect, generosity, and leadership. I've commented on such lists of virtues before. In principle, I support them. In practice, they require a conversion of a certain sort. You can sense that inside yourself, can't you?

I read not long ago that among the most popular programs on television are courtroom shows. Along with reality shows of every type, television programmers want more court programs on their schedule as well. You may have noticed a marked increase in the promotion of such programs and new judges popping up all the time offering Solomonic wisdom in the tones of a sassy, sarcastic, parent-type wearing a black robe. Why the push for these shows? One expert said, "Couch potatoes love to see people get judged. It's fun to see the judge give it to somebody." Actually, I don't think the interest ends with couch potatoes alone. For instance, I noticed, even among those not directly connected with the Oklahoma bombing, the interest in witnessing the execution of Timothy McVeigh for the attack. Desiring to watch people getting it is a more generic human characteristic. And I have this nagging feeling it's not one of our nobler traits.

"Who am I?" I had never heard this question so baldly asked within the first three minutes of an appointment. The middle-aged woman possessed a Ph.D. in physics but had made a career decision for investment banking. Now, having achieved her goals, she awoke one morning with this question looming in her consciousness, and it wouldn't let go. She found the rote, lukewarm religion she had practiced wasn't up to the depth of her angst—it seemed rather childish now. She was a scientist, of course, and though that seemed an adult pursuit, it didn't really respond to her question. She wanted to be able to look into the mirror and see more than the results of a completely random genetic soup. Instinctively she knew there was more to it than this . . . it wasn't simply wishful thinking. No, not wishful thinking, I said, but faith thinking. I added that it was time to embrace a mature religion that matched the mature question she was now asking. The stakes were too high to leave it to either the test tube or childhood residue.

The *Wall Street Journal* reported that a school sent a letter to parents in preparation for teacher conferences. Among the instructions was a strongly worded admonition that said under no circumstances should parents answer a cellular phone during the conference. I assume that means the school has some experience with this. I don't know why it's so hard for us to understand the wisdom of the old overworked adage: actions speak louder than words. We say we really do love our kids, our spouses, our friends, our parents. But in the middle of an important conversation something small interferes, say, the telephone in our pocket rings, and the action of our distracted attention says far more than the words of professed affection. Truth is, the only way children really learn the very important lessons in life, the most important, elemental lessons, is by what adults model for them. They don't hear the words, they absorb the actions.

When I was a young boy, I would scour a stream's edge hunting for frogs. The fun was all in the catching. Once in hand, the frog lost its appeal, so I would grant its freedom and search for yet another willing to give a good chase. Timmy had other ideas. When Timmy caught frogs he liked to squeeze them sideways forcing their wide mouths to open so he could then pour gravel down their throats. I went frogging with Timmy exactly one time. Catch, fill with stones, toss away, cackle with glee, times ten. Though I was inarticulate then, Timmy's actions brought me to a full awareness of the range of choices we humans have, as though a little lightbulb had been turned on in some dark corner. I remember the incident clearly all these many years later. And as the years have passed, I have met my share of adult Timmys who have found far bigger prey than frogs. Just as with that early glimmering, I'm reminded that at every turn in my life, in every moment, small or large, I have choices to make about how I intend to live in the world, and those choices have moral consequence.

Flipping through Sunday's movie ads one would think that the current crop of films is the best ever produced. The reviewers' superlatives gushed. One movie was touted as Wonderful! Outstanding! Engrossing! Inspiring! Superb! Breathtaking! Another film was advertised as "The most powerful film of the year, a knockout of high drama, passionate emotion and electrifying intelligence!" Another was "Brilliantly inventive, boldly imagined, fabulously detailed!" And yet one more was pronounced "A miracle, huge, extraordinary!" Exclamation points everywhere. Evidently this sort of advertising sells films. We're addicted to superlatives, perhaps hoping that a film that is wild and irresistible, dazzling and wonderful just might rub off since we seem to believe life should consist of one breathtaking and utterly original experience after another. It used to be that life was thought to be built on things like Patience! Forbearance! Endurance! Forgiveness! Compassion! What type of movie would help us enjoy more of our real lives? And wouldn't that be wonderful, inspiring, outstanding?

V

My eighteen-year-old son returned from his first semester at college located half across the continent. It was good to see him. I missed having him around. Though at times rather high maintenance, he was very good company and with his leave-taking, like countless parents before me, I wondered where all the years had gone. Though I tried, I could hardly remember holding him in the cradle of one forearm. It was the speed of it all that struck me so—the speed of his growing and the shrinking of time and the wondering if I ever had enough of it for him. I have considered how many times at his asking for my attention I said I didn't have time and now, of course, we don't. Poet Gabriela Mistral is attributed with writing these cautionary words for parents everywhere. "Many things can wait. Children cannot. Today their bones are being formed, their blood is being made, their senses are being developed. To them we cannot say 'tomorrow.' Their name is today."

Over lunch with a student from Columbia University I learned she had just experienced what she thought was a very great failure: she had been rejected at all three graduate programs to which she had applied. She said that all her life she had worked hard, got great grades, but all this rejection made her wonder if she really had anything worthwhile to offer, after all. She was poised on the precipice of despair. I once read a story about a boy who went up in the attic and drew a circle with a big F in the middle because he hadn't been doing well in school, and then hanged himself over the F. His problem was that he didn't distinguish between the grade he was getting and who he was as a person. I shared that with my young friend and told her about a few of my experiences of rejection over the years. And though I'm not usually so adamant in first-time counseling conversations, I told her never, ever, to hand over her essential identity to anyone other than the God who loved her beyond her wildest imaginings.

I was in charge of the ten-year-old. We were waiting for the city bus to whisk him off to school. Passing the time, he eagerly told me about all the different ways he and his friends scammed the bus drivers to get a free ride. They used expired bus passes; they passed a single card between them so it was used multiple times; they set up elaborate games of distraction; and so on. Especially since I knew money was not an issue for him and his friends, I asked why they did it. He answered with his own question, "Why should we pay when we can get away with it for free?" Feeling like a teaching moment had arrived, I explained that in order for the city to have buses in the first place, it required all citizens to share the burden of the cost, and paying a small fare was the price. He said, "Yeah, I know, but *still,* if I can get away with it, why shouldn't I?" I spent the rest of the morning thinking about his question. I knew it was an age-appropriate moral conundrum for him, but I wondered just how many adults had ever actually learned the answer.

Perhaps you know this story of challenging inspiration. It bears repeating. Anna Mary Robertson worked as a "hired girl" on a farm. She met and married a hired hand on that farm by the name of Tom Moses. They moved to a farm of their own and raised ten children. Anna loved to do needlework, but as she became older, her hands stiffened with arthritis. So she decided to try painting and found she could handle the paintbrush more easily. One day an art collector passed through her small town and saw her paintings in a drugstore. She had been discovered—at seventy-seven years of age. She continued to paint until several months before her death at 101. Why do we now have the wonderful paintings by Grandma Moses? Her hands were too stiff to embroider. Have you been thinking that maybe you are too old, too young, too poor, too much in pain, too anything at all to get unstuck from your present circumstance? Choice is a powerful human tool. Perhaps the most powerful there is. And the beauty of it is, it's available to everyone.

A teacher in Piper, Kansas, found that nearly a fourth of her high school sophomores had cheated on a major botany project, and she gave all of them a zero for their efforts, which meant they faced failing the semester. After parents complained, the school board ordered the teacher to raise their grades. She resigned in protest. At least a dozen of the school's faculty planned to resign in support of their peer. "It's not just biology, you're teaching them a lot more than that," she was reported to have said at the time. "You're teaching them to be honest people, to have integrity, to listen, to be good citizens." After the school board forced the grade reconsideration, one student told her, "We won." Which is reminiscent of the aphorism about winning the battle but losing the war. I wonder what the complaining parents might say if they held stock in Enron.

If you were to ask my wife she'd tell you that I have a pathetic inability to find things around the house. She routinely catches me like a deer in headlights gazing into a closet completely oblivious to the thing I'm looking for which is right in front of my face. In the first days of our marriage she believed I was just lazy. But as the years progressed it began to dawn on her that the more likely cause of my blindness had to do with a certain genetic deficiency. But then looking through a cupboard for a screwdriver is one thing; rummaging in the territory of our personalities is quite another. You know how this is—the person with whom you live sees you with a very different set of eyes than you see yourself. You can stare into the mirror for hours and still not see the patently obvious neuroses that your partner sees in you. I think I'm blind in this way, too, and it has nothing to do with unique genetics. The only comfort I have in this is that I'm quite certain I share this disability with everyone who reads these words. A small comfort at that.

Through quiet tears Mary told me about another
failed relationship. Now forty and nearly desperate
to find the right partner, she questioned that it would
ever happen. She had always believed there was just one
person who was her true soul mate. Each of her
relationships started out well, but at some point each fell
flat. There always came that day when she awakened to
the feeling she was no longer in love. What was wrong
with her? Mary asked. I told her I had no idea if
anything was wrong. But I did know that even if she
ever were to find her true soul mate, so-called, there
would inevitably come the day she would roll over in bed
and think to herself, "What on earth am I doing here?"
Then, I added, would come her opportunity to discover
what love was more nearly about, because at that
moment she would have to *choose* to love or not. Though
we're allergic to this truth, love really has a lot to do with
choice. We would rather think of it as something that
happens *to us* than as something that is created *by us*. I
think this allergy helps explain why there's so little of it
in our world and how easy it is to lose.

If you're like I am, there are times in your life when you feel discouraged, maybe even defeated by your current circumstance. Though we might wish otherwise, life inevitably presents us with a relentless series of challenges. We've heard and vaguely remember the admonitions about perseverance and clichés like, "When the going gets tough, the tough get going." But then, sometimes these ring hollow in ears tuned by cynicism. I was recently reminded about the story of Ray Kroc, a relatively lackluster marketer of restaurant equipment, who didn't sell his first hamburger until the age of fifty-two. At a time when many start thinking about retirement, Kroc turned McDonald's into the world's largest fast food restaurant. Now, I don't share that exact dream, but I do find it hopeful to consider that I'm arriving at his lift-off age. This makes me realize that every day, even the ones that fall on this side of bleak, inevitably give way to tomorrow, and tomorrow is a brand-spanking-new day.

It was the summer after my sophomore year in high school, 1968. My brother was home from the Air Force Academy, and we wandered into a brand new, big screen, cinemascope blockbuster called *2001: A Space Odyssey*. I can't say what exactly happened to me in the theater that night, but I left different than when I entered. Not quite sixteen years old, I was ripe for a kick-in-the-head experience that would awaken my capacity to think. And this movie was just the ticket. Already an active reader, ideas began to capture and excite my attention as never before. That fall an English teacher picked up on my newfound mental agitation and rose to his mentoring heights in planting the seeds that kept this young man thinking right through the millennial threshold. I became a fan of science fiction, which in turn spurred an interest in novels and nonfiction of every sort. Through the alchemy of a raw, awakened mind and the commitment of a mentor, I was set on a path of lifelong learning. Not long ago I awoke from a deep, satisfying sleep aware of this memory and grateful for my mental mentors. So here's to teachers everywhere who do their jobs well. Thanks to all of you for the crucial service you perform. I'm guessing you don't hear that nearly enough.

I talian scientists reported the discovery of a gene that exerts major control over the life span of mice. This seems a dubious accomplishment given our more natural inclination to shorten the life span of mice. But these scientists explain that mice are quite similar to people at the genetic level. Thus, much longer-lived mice could lead to much longer-lived humans. Which also has a smell of the dubious about it, considering the explosive growth rate of the human population. Newborns depend upon the willingness of their forebears to vacate the scene in a timely fashion. Of course, the quest for the fountain of youth has been the dream of narcissists forever and depending upon the birthday, I suppose I could count myself among them. Still, the question that hangs in the air when considering the prospect of an additional twenty years, is just what are we doing with the current twenty? If only the scientists could find the gene that helps us focus on the present.

The young man had been caught in a series of lies. He had lost his job as a result and his marriage was in serious crisis. He said he didn't know why he had done it. Well, on the short run he *did* know—he wanted to get ahead and he wanted life on his terms. He shared that he had been raised in a religious household, was taught the Ten Commandments, but truthfully, they seemed rather quaint and irrelevant in the world into which he had graduated. Being honest was simply a tool that one used when it was convenient and discarded when it wasn't. It was fortunate, I thought, that his current crisis had caught him at this early stage. I don't know if cynicism or narcissism or some grand alchemy of the two is our biggest problem today. Venerable George Washington once said, "I hope I shall possess firmness and virtue enough to maintain what I consider the most enviable of all titles, the character of an honest man." That this sounds so out of step with today's culture greatly disturbs me.

The noisy man finally sat down. I was attending a
board meeting of a not-for-profit organization
considering an important strategic vision and we had
just heard a lengthy rant from a prominent member who
thought himself the brightest star in the room. This
particular individual, though very smart and successful
in business, displayed personal values that were clearly
at odds with the values of the organization we were all
supposed to be advancing. His commandeering our
process was threatening to undo years of painstaking
work. Here's an essential dilemma of our time: which do
we value more, success or character? Often they seem
pitched against each other. Though both have their
merit, I can't help but feel Dostoyevsky had it right
when he wrote, "It's not the brains that matter most, but
that which guides them—the character, the heart,
generous qualities, progressive ideas."

Some years ago the *Wall Street Journal* ran a story concerning the Texas Rangers' "Career Development Program," which was designed to teach its ballplayers about manners, etiquette, decorum, and character. As Scott McCartney reported, "With professional sports scandals becoming as common as mustard on hot dogs, more teams are offering player-education programs to protect their million-dollar investments, bolster sportsmanship and win back fans." Not a bad idea. Professional sports could use some rehabilitation. One practical tip: make sure you drop your beer bottle—a potential weapon—when accosted by a drunk intent on picking a fight with a baseball star. As one of the instructors said, "Say 400,000 youngsters are looking up to you, think what an opportunity you'd have. Being a good role model in the community is part of being a Ranger." How refreshing that sounds. But I think we need to expand this program beyond sports.

Parents of young children juggle the pressures of career and family life with varying degrees of success. Most will organize their lives in ways that pay attention to milestone events like birthdays, but I observe that parents often miss the fact that important times with kids generally happen in small moments and in small ways that can't actually be planned. A walk to the store or a bedtime conversation can mean more than a lifetime of expensive, well-executed birthday parties. Musing about life's high points, Susan B. Anthony is often quoted as saying: "Sooner or later we all discover that the important moments in life are not the advertised ones, not the birthdays, the graduations, the weddings, not the great goals achieved. The real milestones are less prepossessing. They come to the door of memory unannounced, stray dogs that amble in, sniff around a bit, and simply never leave. Our lives are measured by these." There's wisdom here for parents. Nothing creates relationship like shared, unplanned time. This comes more as a result of attitude and lifestyle, and not so much by marking the calendar once in a while.

VI

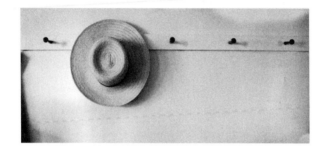

My four-year-old son loved to imitate me as I worked in the yard. He particularly liked the huge pruning shears and was frustrated by my keeping them stored well out of reach. Returning home one day, I discovered a row of flowers, once two-feet tall, had been neatly clipped to a few inches of their lives. Running to the back of the house I discovered that now lying among the recent trimmings were six stalks of unusual lilies I highly prized. I checked the basement and found the not-so-carefully stacked boards and boxes leading to the forbidden, and now missing, scissors. Emerging outside, I saw my son with shears outstretched, framed by the sun, like some mighty gladiator standing defiant among the defeated. I was furious. Everywhere the flowers had been decapitated. But the following spring, rather than six stalks of lilies, twelve sprang up. I took my son outside; we sat on the porch steps and taught each other something about pruning and loving and disciplining and miracles.

At church one Sunday I spied a young boy standing off by himself looking rather bereft. I went over to him and introduced myself. I asked him his name. He told me his name was "Stupid." I said I couldn't believe that was his real name. But he quickly retorted that I could believe what I wanted, but his name was "Stupid" because that's what everyone called him. Said with a quiet finality, he strode away. Later, I spotted him on his way out the door with a man I believe was his father. I don't know what preceded this exact moment, but I witnessed his father turning a very ugly face toward his son and hissing, "My God, you are just so *stupid*!" The boy glanced up and caught my eye for a long moment, then shrugged his shoulders and walked out the door. That happened a lot of years ago. In the meantime I've witnessed far worse behaviors. Still, I've never forgotten the knowing look in the boy's eyes and the pain and insight we shared for just a moment.

The news report began this way: "An eighty-two-year-old Nassau County man whose sport utility vehicle collided with a minivan full of young soccer players on a Long Island highway, killing him and two of the children, had a level of alcohol in his system that was more than twice the legal limit ..." The story described the shock and grief of the families and the boys' delightful personalities. This brought to mind the numbers of persons who have passed through my office in a state of deep grief. Much of the time the loss was due to causes beyond their control and their emotional task consisted mainly of acceptance of the new reality. But sometimes the grief was due to causes that were very much within human control; and those agonies were the more difficult to process, for there the personal work involved the realm of moral culpability as, for instance, it might be imbedded within a decision as simple as whether or not to turn the key in the ignition.

Something of a dramatic morality drama unfolded in Cambridge, Massachusetts, that played live on television. It concerned the trial of a father charged with manslaughter in the beating death of another father during a practice hockey game. A medical examiner testified that the fatal injury was caused by enormous force and that the victim's head was almost severed from his neck. Ironically, the defendant claimed his agitation was sparked by his perception that the other father was encouraging rough play during the pickup game in which the defendant's ten-year-old boy was playing. I wonder what lessons the boys will take from this episode. I also wonder what lessons adults will take. Experience tells me that most of us most of the time act in ways that are consistent with our individual habits of heart and mind. This got me to wondering what habits the two fathers practiced, which provided more than enough distraction from considering my own.

The young actress (there are a lot of young actors in the city) said to me, "Sometimes I get tired trying to live up to my own best intentions and feel like throwing in the towel. Life would be easier then … just surrender to the forces that drag me down." I responded that I had felt that way myself a time or two. Why indeed hold to certain standards when the world seems indifferent? These words of Martin Luther King Jr. provide a sober assessment of the situation: "We have just so much strength in us. If we give and give and give—after a while, at a certain point, we're so weak and worn, we hoist up the flag of surrender. We surrender to the worst side of ourselves. We surrender to self-pity and to spite and to morose self-preoccupation. If you want to call it depression or burnout, well, all right. If you want to call it the triumph of sin—when our goodness has been knocked out from under us, well, all right. Whatever we say or think, this is arduous duty, doing this kind of work; to live out one's idealism brings with it hazards." When we're down, it's good to have reliable role models, and it is very good to have friends who value the same things we do.

I officiated at the wedding of a young man I've known for most of his life. I've been present to his maturation. I've also come to know the woman he married. I feel very good about them. The wedding was supposed to take place on a lovely lawn beside the ocean, but the weather was sour with driving rain so we moved indoors—only the first such adjustment to reality they will face together. Among the words read during the ceremony was this phrase written by Saint Paul: "When I was a child, I spoke like a child, I thought like a child, I reasoned like a child; when I became an adult, I put an end to childish ways." This follows Paul's thoughts about love being patient and kind, never envious or arrogant, etc., which in turn prompted my musing about what an audaciously adult activity a marriage really is today and how strangely hard it seems to be an "adult." The majority of us make it there chronologically, but experience reveals fewer of us arrive emotionally. On the other hand, knowing that faith, hope, and love do abide, it's never too late to give it a shot.

I recently read that in 1905 Albert Schweitzer turned from his well-established and highly accomplished career in philosophy, music, and theology, to medicine, so he could work in Africa on behalf of the Paris Missionary Society. Explaining this decision he wrote, "For years I have been giving of myself in words"; he no longer wished to talk a good game, but to live authentically. "My life is my argument," is how he came to summarize his decision. This stark statement caught me up short, caused me to think for a moment about what the content of my life argued for. Apart from the words I speak (after all, I'm in a profession of great talkers), what did the content of my life actually reveal? The Letter of James (2:18) in the New Testament says this: "I by my works will show you my faith." That's patently obvious when I apply it to others. As always, the trick is in the self-application, and quite frankly, I'm less good at that.

The young man in my office was fidgety, uncertain of why he had come. He was well dressed, very put-together. He had questions, he said. He was confused. Offering a seat, I asked him what he did for a living. He told me he was a successful Wall-Streeter. Very successful. Only thirty-two years old, he had already accumulated a large fortune. He now had everything he had ever dreamed of wanting. His problem, he said, was now that he had it all, he didn't much care. This feeling surprised him and disturbed him, *deeply* disturbed him. He considered finding a therapist, but for some reason decided to check in with a minister first—he didn't really know why. After a bit more conversation I gave him some homework and suggested he come back in a week after pondering these words of Evelyn Underhill: "We mostly spend our lives conjugating three verbs: to Want, to Have and to Do." We miss the one verb with any real significance, she says—to be! A year and a half later, we're still having that conversation. We've both learned a lot.

The lack of leisure time has become a serious health threat, as pointed out in the *Utne Reader*. Mark Harris reports that according to the Surgeon General, about one in four American adults reports no leisure-time activity, and the Bureau of Labor reports an average married couple works 26 percent longer each year than couples did thirty years ago. In addition, a University of Michigan study found that "real" free time among children ages twelve and under declined from 40 percent in 1981 to 25 percent in 1997. Harris remarks ironically that "Fifty years ago, commentators wondered what we were going to do with all the extra leisure time generated by the 'automation revolution.'" Actually, many of us are now working about a month more per year than was the norm in the 1960s, he says. I know many of you suspected this must be so. How else to account for the unrelenting stress, sleep disorders, and exhaustion? I know work is important. But so is play. Why not take tomorrow off and have some fun for a change? And while you're at it, take the kids.

In his book *Life After God*, Generation X novelist Douglas Coupland says this: "I have never really felt like I was 'from' anywhere; home to me ... is a shared electronic dream of cartoon memories, half-hour sitcoms and national tragedies. I have always prided myself on my lack of accent—my lack of any discernible regional flavor. I used to think mine was a Pacific Northwest accent, from where I grew up, but then I realized my accent was simply the accent of nowhere—the accent of a person who has no fixed home in their mind." There's a certain wistfulness in this statement. To my mind, to have no fixed home is to have no fixed relationships. No "people." He wrote his generational reflection in 1994. It would be interesting to check in with him now to see how his life and opinion have evolved. Experience reveals that "home" materializes as a result of specific, robust commitments. I'm wondering how this generation called "X" will find and make theirs.

The man sat across from me in my office. He appeared to be the very model of parental care. He told me how much he loved his son. How very much he wanted to help him. He spoke glowingly about sacrifice and commitment. I actually thought he was eloquent. Then I spoke to his son the next day. He told of an abusive household, where physical and verbal violence were the norm. He told of the difficulty he had in making others believe his highly successful and highly regarded father was, in fact, a scared bully. In Orson Scott Card's novel, *Alvin Journeyman,* a wise storyteller asks a hypocritical young man this question: "Where do you draw the line between a humble man who knows his own weaknesses but tries to act out virtues he hasn't quite mastered yet, and a proud man who pretends to have those virtues without the slightest intention of acquiring them?" Hypocrisy is the most pernicious of human failings. It hides us from ourselves and through it we wreak havoc. I'm not sure how we overcome the powerful, nearly addictive desire to play masquerade. I guess we just have to want to, plain and simple.

While walking to work one morning I was lost in deep thought. Only semiconscious of my surroundings, I stepped off the curb into the street as a car was making a left turn. It screeched to a halt just inches from my knees, and like a startled deer, I managed to look up in stupefaction, stunned and uncomprehending. The driver of what I now saw was a big Mercedes with darkened windows, leaned out of his open window and screamed a string of deafening epithets, paused, and concluded with a well-punctuated, "Go to hell!" Now I think I'm a reasonably thick-skinned person, but that particular day I was caught off guard by the violence in the man who nearly ran me down. In fact, I rather suspect he wished he had. I know, because sometimes I've been sitting in the same seat, if not the very same car. Funny, how when I'm behind the wheel, pedestrians are annoying as hell, but when I'm walking it's the drivers who ought to have their licenses revoked. Have you ever noticed that annoying irony?

Elliot was on the horns of a dilemma. A sophomore in high school, Elliot had knowledge that a certain classmate everyone detested had been falsely accused of stealing $150 from a teacher's purse. He was not the thief—Elliot saw his friend take the money. Was loyalty or truth more important? He didn't know what to do. As we talked together, Elliot said that it would be easiest to do nothing. There was nothing that associated him with knowledge about the crime. He could stay free and clear of the problem. M. Scott Peck has written, "Problems are the cutting edge that distinguishes between success and failure. Problems call forth our courage and our wisdom; indeed, they create our courage and our wisdom." I suggested to Elliot that the easy way out was often the worst way out and that maybe he needed to live with his problem for a while. It would be uncomfortable, but I would help him hold it.

I was accompanying my ten-year-old to a friend's house uptown. I said we would take the subway. Stephanie was adamant about taking a taxi. The cost differential was considerable. One of us sulking and the other crabby, we tramped down the subway stairwell and stood in disagreeable silence until the train arrived. One stop down line Stephanie respectfully suggested we weren't traveling in the right direction. Thinking she was "sharing an attitude" about taking the train I snapped back, "Of course we are!" But by the next stop I realized she was right. Before the doors closed I barked that we had better get off, and a gloriously expansive grin spread across her beaming face. We darted up the stairs and hailed a cab. No words were exchanged between us until we arrived at the door of her friend's house when Stephanie quietly said, "You know, Dad, you never listen to me." On my way home I thought about that and decided, grudgingly, she had a point ... maybe I didn't listen to her very well. I've been working on that ever since. Of course, we take the train whenever possible.

VII

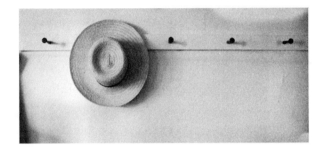

After the shock and revulsion wore off, a great wave of sadness washed over me as I heard of the horrible starvation death of the four-year-old girl, whose parents had been "disciplining" her. I prayed for her. And then I felt I should include her five sisters and brothers—and yes, even her mother and father. At that moment I was filled only with a very great sorrow. I surprised myself when my prayer continued for my own children, and then for my wife and myself. A self-centered response, perhaps, but it felt like a hedge against ... starvation. There are so many different hungers and so many starving children and adults in our land. It's tempting when such a contemptible tragedy occurs to publicly vilify, even crucify, the wrongdoers. Surely justice has needs that must be met, but probably a more useful response for most of us would be to attend to the various hungers within our own families, and to then consider how families together share a community, a city, a nation, a world.

I recently asked a young computer whiz and game aficionado to give me a tutorial on the current state of video and computer games. In particular, I was interested in the notorious "Grand Theft Auto," which has figured in the defense of a couple of young men accused of assault, rape, and murder. I wanted to experience it for myself. What I discovered was a very cleverly designed environment where the gamer must break the law, kill cops, stomp on the heads of prostitutes, and generally wreak havoc. I confess that I felt the seduction of playing on the dark side, and while I believe only a truly damaged individual would act out that virtual scenario in the real world, I was disturbed by my own response to the role-play. And I got to wondering about the millions of kids who play it while plugged in to gangsta rap on their iPods and MP3 players, and I wondered about parents and families, and the nurture of bonds of deep human community, and I thought how fragile they are, really, and how crucially important. And I realized that a game built on those values would not sell. And I wondered some more.

At the age of twenty-three, Chad Pregracke had become disgusted by the trash and debris accumulating in his beloved Mississippi River, along which shores he had grown up. One day he said he would take it upon himself to do something about it. Snubbed by the state of Illinois, he started up the Mississippi River Beautification and Restoration Project. That first summer he single-handedly picked up forty-five thousand pounds of trash in a hundred-mile stretch. His success led to donations and help. Six years later the project's budget rose to more than two hundred thousand dollars, and many individuals and businesses committed to clean up specific stretches of the river regularly. His success caused him to move on to other rivers. Makes one think the following is right, which is widely attributed to Margaret Mead: "Never doubt that a small group of thoughtful, committed citizens can change the world; indeed, it's the only thing that ever has."

I visited the Holocaust Museum in Washington, D.C., shortly after it opened. I will never forget this first visit. Though I had been profoundly moved in museums before, I had never wept in one. Was it the shoes of the victims that first brought my stomach to my throat? The visitor is invited to interact, to see, to touch, to hear, the vicious human evil that should never be forgotten. The space was full of people who were strangely quiet and attentive, wakeful and vital. There were no sleepwalkers, no reluctant spouses trailing with tired ambivalence. No, the displays could not be avoided. They demanded attention. Author Chaim Potok suggests that "It takes an immense measure of courage to enter a museum which is not about beauty but about grim and profound truths concerning the more appalling aspects of humankind. That so many millions of people are prepared to encounter this very different kind of museum is a clear testament of hope for our species." Count yourself among those courageous persons. Add your soul to the community of hope. Among the city's monuments to vainglory and courage, this one adds a solemn counterpoint that brings necessary depth and breadth to understanding our human experience.

New Yorker cartoon by Jack Zielger entitled, "A Courtesy Call," depicts a crazed man on the telephone listening to a voice proclaim, "Please remain on hold while we complete the final details of the theft of your identity," which captures the sense of threat I've been experiencing over this newest of mass perversities. If paranoia is the intended result of large-scale marketing campaigns and ubiquitous news reports concerning identity theft, I think it's working. I guess I'm supposed to be more vigilant in protecting myself from these nameless, faceless mass robbers. Although, besides frequently checking my credit report, little else seems available in my defense. All the while, everyone with whom I do business wants my social security number. That's what it all boils down to these days—a series of numbers and presto! one's identity is right there for the taking! This evokes the sinking feeling that our identities have been up for grabs for some time. Between you and me, I don't think a credit check will help much if that's true.

The immaculate courtroom was bereft of all
ornamentation save one: the large raised letters above
the head of the judge that read, *In God We Trust*. Serving on
my first jury, I was surprised to find this prominent
historical artifact and wondered what my co-jurors might
have thought about it. There's no doubt that the structures
of our democracy were initially built upon transcendent
principles. The concept of "God," variously described, has
been behind the curtains of our legal system from its
inception. But this philosophical/theological construct is
under increasing scrutiny, ironically at a time when issues of
morality, ethics, and values in government and all cultural
environments are being raised into high relief. Awash in a
cacophony of shrill voices, we seem to have lost much of our
ability to think and speak deeply about how these matters
intersect and how all of us are held accountable to principles
that are much larger than our individual desires. Just what
does bind together a diverse nation into a healthy, robust
community? Surprised, I found jury duty not a bad place to
think about this. Not a bad place at all.

If you come to New York City, I highly recommend making the short ferry trip to Ellis Island. This is a fascinating place. Between 1892 and 1924, twenty-two million immigrants passed through on their way to a new life in America. On a recent visit I learned that only the folks who couldn't afford first- or second-class passage across the Atlantic had to process through Ellis Island, basically those who traveled steerage. I also learned that far from being motivated by altruism, Ellis Island was the invention of the steamship companies for whom passage to the United States was a very profitable business. Which isn't to say that the millions of persons didn't benefit from this arrangement. Obviously many more millions of us are the direct beneficiaries of that human supply and demand proposition that made New York Harbor the emblem of freedom and opportunity. Seems strange to me how we North Americans so value our history of being the land that welcomed the tired, the poor, the huddled masses yearning to breathe free and yet continuously struggle with accepting new groups as they arrive. One historical fact should help: none of us really has any prior claim to the land except those who were here in the first place.

I met Dan at an agency for homeless teenagers. I knew this full-time volunteer had achieved a high level of success in banking only to take a year's leave to work with kids. Late one night I asked him why. Dan said it came down to an exchange with his boss one Friday afternoon. Dan had promised himself he would spend Saturday with his two sons whom he rarely saw and sorely missed. His boss said an important meeting had been called for ten the next morning. Dan replied he had promised the day to his boys. His boss immediately shot back that if Dan wished to stay part of the team he'd have to change his attitude. If he was really serious about his career, his boys would have to raise themselves. However, Dan would be the best damn provider they could ever want or need! Dan said that when it was put to him that way, his decision was really quite easy. His life issues had never been in sharper focus. He was grateful for the opportunity to say that on Saturday he would be playing hardball on another field.

I returned home exhausted after an especially tough work day which had begun with an early morning news report instructing me on how, in the event of a chemical or biological attack, I could seal up my windows with duct tape and plastic, store water, and secure a survival kit ranging in price from fifty-nine dollars to over two thousand dollars. The city was very jittery. Police sirens whipped around my building all day. Tired from anxiety and work, I clicked on the television just as a reality-based show was airing: *Are You Hot?* I watched for a moment as beautiful young women and men paraded before three judges for their numerical opinion on the matter. Then I turned it off, sat quietly, and recalled a fragment of wisdom said to be from Jesuit Pierre Teilhard de Chardin: "We are collaborators in creation. What you and I are becoming, the world is becoming." I thought I then heard the ring of truth, followed immediately by the blast of an alarm.

The middle-aged man sitting in my office said he was depressed. Nothing had gone right for him over the last number of years. His third marriage had failed. He went on and on about all the problems of his former wife. His career was in a shambles. He complained he had never landed a position where his real talents were put to good use. People always underestimated his various abilities. It was no wonder he couldn't achieve his goals, he said, people thwarted him at every turn. I asked if he ever seriously talked with anyone about these issues. He said no. He didn't believe in counselors and therapists. A Zen saying goes something like, "When the gentleman archer misses his mark, he looks inward"— meaning that the target isn't at fault. Archers know that to improve their aim, they must improve themselves. Evidently that was an important bit of wisdom that had been left out of my visitor's education.

Am I alone in my dislike of the crawler that has appeared at the bottom of news channels these days? It seems that nearly all have jumped on board with this formatting technique. Did producers think we weren't already getting enough information? Was it the success of Bloomberg's method of delivering moment-by-moment updates in the financial markets? Am I the only one who finds it bit bizarre to be viewing, say, the carnage in Iraq as the gross take for *Harry Potter* scrolls by underneath? I guess the point is that all of it is just information. In this sense, nothing is inherently more important than anything else. "All information is equal" would seem to be the new motto. And the more the better. I suppose it could be a sign of age, although in fact, I'm not very old. But perhaps old enough to still believe that some information can't really be absorbed without a certain amount of time and focus and deserves a respectful attentiveness.

Whenever I hear that the organization of which I'm a part, that is, the institutional church, has decided to reorganize, I wince. Not that I'm opposed to change, mind you. In fact, I support change, long for change. It's just that over time I've become a tad cynical whenever I hear that an encrusted bureaucratic system wants to change itself. I recently came across this observation: "We trained hard—but it seemed that every time we were beginning to form into teams, we would be reorganized. I was to learn later in life that we tend to meet any new situation by re-organizing; and a wonderful method it can be for creating the illusion of progress, while producing confusion, inefficiency and demoralization." This is said to have been written in A.D. 71 by the Roman, Gaius Petronius. Sounds strangely modern, doesn't it? Notwithstanding the success of the four-star blockbuster movie *Titanic* some years ago, we seem impervious to the parable concerning the rearrangement of deck chairs. I suppose it's easier to concern ourselves with the trivial when crises loom large.

There's no question that security has been raised to priority number one for most Americans. And there's no question that we'll be spending a lot more for it in the years ahead. A lot more of our gross national product will be devoted to new programs, personnel, and weapons to provide a supposedly better version of security. We'll try to export the problem to distant lands. For those lucky enough to live in the wealthiest nation, until the dawning of the twenty-first century we've managed to protect such decisions as whether to eat French or Italian tonight, watch *Sex and the City* or *Law and Order,* take in a ball game, or brood upon which SUV best meets the demands of the urban pioneer. Yet, a pesky truth sneaks in between the cracks of these decisions, with its silent testimony that human striving is unable to provide the comfort and security we most deeply desire. And we have a sneaking suspicion that all the bombs in the world can't protect us to the degree we fantasize. Is it possible there is something stronger than a war machine of unparalleled power that can provide the most resilient defense?

Politicians and economists remind us that capitalism allows the most individuals the greatest levels of personal freedom. Assuming that's true, it's interesting how many persons say they are dissatisfied with what the free market offers, say, within the various media for instance. But it's important to remember that television and radio programming, movies, videos, and the World Wide Web are handled and marketed in the same way as soap and toilet paper—it's all supply and demand. Within our market system we can hardly complain that we get what we ask for. The market gives us what we want, without regard for what we, or our children, may actually need. We may complain about lousy television fare, for instance, or the ubiquity of Internet pornography, but it stands to reason that lots of folks are tuning in. It bears repeating that freedom and responsibility go hand in hand. The superstructure upon which freedom hangs is made of the routine decisions and choices that each one of us makes day in and day out—the same way individual character is built.

everal friends were having a heated after-dinner discussion concerning the development and promulgation of certain values within our culture. A variety of opinions were shared, but all of them displayed concern for the future. Sitting quietly throughout was a young man, fifteen years old, who finally blurted out that he attended a prestigious private school with the children of powerful families, and if they reflected the future of values in our nation, then we were in deep trouble. His passionate outburst brought us to silence. In his book *The Chosen,* author Chaim Potok depicts a father's recollections of his early years with his son. "A *heart* I need for a son, a *soul* I need for a son, *compassion* I want from my son, righteousness, mercy, strength to suffer and to carry pain, *that* I want from my son, not a mind without a soul!" My friends and I set to wondering where that sort of education was taking place. At home? School? After what was it being modeled? Parents? Government? Teachers? The fundamental infrastructure of our national life is built person by person. Just who's doing the building—and how?

VIII

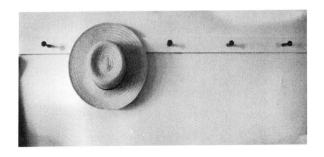

The young man told me he felt stuck. He had returned home after college and now five years later was still living there feeling as though he had accomplished none of what he said he would. He got along well with his folks—they liked having him around. But his life was on hold. He had developed no really deep relationships, and no real life direction. He wanted many things, but the truth was, they seemed hard to get, and he was afraid of failure. I said that it sounded like he wanted to stay stuck, despite his protestations. Was he willing to risk or not? Without risking some pain, he would have to live his life without many things: marriage, children, even abiding friendship, not to mention fulfilled dreams of satisfied accomplishment— anything that was bound to provide him with meaning and contentment. I remember my father telling me, "Steve, pain's a part of life." Somewhere, somehow, that simple truth sunk in, which it must if we're to live lives worthy of the gift. No one can ultimately give this perspective to another, but we can repeat it like my father did, hoping that one day it will finally take root.

*H*ope *Magazine* reported that one of ten finalists for a
Volvo Life Award was an eighty-eight-year-old
woman named Thelma Harrison. About fifteen years
ago, or when she was in her seventy-third year, this
great-great-grandmother founded the "Mama, I Want to
Read" preschool initiative in one of Norfolk, Virginia's
poorest neighborhoods. This free program preps
children for kindergarten by teaching them their ABCs,
their addresses and phone numbers, how to count to one
hundred, how to dress, tie their shoes, and other
fundamentals. "I saw a need for this," she says. "In this
community many mothers are on welfare. They don't
have an education. They need this help with their
children." The man who nominated her said that
Thelma's "greatest love in life is helping others to help
themselves." Kind of makes you think a bit differently
about the whole idea of retirement, doesn't it? For that
matter, it makes you think about what really matters
right now, whatever your age happens to be.

I don't know if it's good news or bad. Scientists recently reported that contrary to established wisdom, the onslaught of puberty may actually begin around the age of six. Evidence suggests that like most other aspects of human development, sexuality is more a process than an event that hits around the age of thirteen. And scientists now say that process begins in middle childhood with a shift in hormone balances. Come to think of it, this would account for my infatuation with my fourth-grade teacher, Miss Coy, whose name had a striking resonance with her manner. I don't know whether this window into human maturation will lead to any breakthroughs in medicine, teaching, or parenting, but with it I'm reminded how very little we really know about many things. What I long for is the day our scientists can provide a bit of wisdom on why our culture is infatuated with fully developed adults who act out with about the same amount of maturity as six year olds. Now that would be a real breakthrough.

The twentieth-century psychiatrist Carl Jung commented that among his patients in the second half of life, all of them had fallen ill because they had lost what the living religions of every age have given their followers. The spiritual background—taught in primitive tribes as well as in highly differentiated civilizations—has gone astray, Jung explained. "Our Christian doctrine has lost its grip to an appalling extent," he said. "People are no more rooted in their world and lose their orientation. They just drift. That is very much our condition, too ... life loses its meaning ... The problem itself cannot be settled by a few slogans. It demands concentrated attention, much mental work and, above all, patience, the rarest thing in our restless and crazy time." That's how he described the human circumstance in 1959, a time we hardly consider crazy. Even a casual observer now would see that the situation of slogans addressing questions of meaning has reached absurd proportions. Where can people go to find something more lasting, something far more substantive than the thin gruel served in popular culture? How can people find their true orientation? Hmmm.

Living in these early years of the twenty-first century, none of us is immune to the effects of the staggering potential of human ingenuity in science and technology. Yet for all of the impending material changes, it's worth considering whether or not human nature also has changed. In a newspaper interview at the time of the millennial cusp, Harvard scientist and student of human nature Edward O. Wilson was asked about this. He responded that it's safe to say that human nature has not changed in the last one hundred thousand years and there's no reason to think it will change in the next one thousand. Here's what caught my attention especially: it's his scientific premise that the "predisposition to religious belief is the most complex and powerful force in the human mind and that the conflict over the origin of humanity and ethics will be the struggle for the human soul in the twenty-first century." This is a struggle over who or what is the source of our ingenuity, who or what owns our souls. After reading his considered opinion I thought to myself, "That will preach well beyond my retirement."

P BS aired a program concerning the Truth and
Reconciliation Commission in South Africa that
was established to help restore a portion of justice. The
show was difficult to watch because of the painful
testimonies of apartheid's destructiveness and graphic
examples that detailed the techniques of torture and
killing that were employed. The program tested the level
of how much truth we can take. One could not watch
and not consider the ultimate ramifications of virulent
racism and its relatives. Think South Africa. Think
Kosovo. Think Rwanda. Think about U.S. history
(slavery, lynchings, the Civil Rights struggle). If we're
brave, we learn the germs of this disease are in all of us.
Bishop Desmond Tutu, chairman of the Commission,
asserted, "[T]his is a moral universe, and you've got to
take account of the fact that truth and lies and goodness
and evil are things that matter, and we've got to
acknowledge them." If we do live in a moral universe,
then we cannot evade the truth. So in principle, I agree
with him. But I also know I'm an expert at evasion.

Columnist George Will reported that while repairing a stone floor of an outside sculpture exhibit at a museum of fine arts, construction workers cordoned off a bronze sculpture with a velvet rope and protected it with burlap and duct tape. The wind uncovered a corner of the burlap and exposed a third of the sculpture. The construction crew overheard what some visitors saw in this. Writes Will, "For about half an hour they discussed the deep symbolism and implication of the artist having covered his work in burlap and why he allowed the public only partial access to what was there. They waxed long and hard about the appropriateness of the texture of the burlap in relation to the medium used. And what the use of the velvet rope meant in juxtaposition to the base of the burlap and duct tape. And the cosmic significance of using degradable materials to hide the true inner beauty." The old saying suggests that "beauty is in the eye of the beholder." But then sometimes beholders don't really know what they're talking about, do they?

A friend deeply attuned to market machinations called in a bleary depression and awakened me late in the night. Did I see how bad things were going to get? Could I see we were heading into an international depression? Did I understand how the president's mess kept us leaderless at a most crucial moment? I was the chosen vessel to receive the morose diatribe of a man highly invested in his investments. The sky was falling, all was lost. Alas. I didn't know if his dire predictions were accurate. Since I was only a modest investor, I was surprised he called me with his analysis. But later I realized that though he had no relationship with my church, the "reverend thing" prompted his call. He was scared; his fear dredged up the questions of meaning. By instinct he knew that though I was no expert at predicting what the next months would bring by way of politics and economics, I was very certain that long after our Congress sputtered its last word and the market was spent, matters of the soul and spirit would endure. That's why I got the call. His instincts were good. That came to me after he hung up. I prayed for him, and I fell into a deep sleep.

William Butler Yeats wrote his famous poem, "The Second Coming," in 1920, a time when most people assumed that what had just come to an end was "the war to end all wars." Yeats sensed, however, that the new political and cultural configurations were wildly unstable. There was no unifying principle, or cause, that could bind nations and peoples together. He seemed the prophet by suggesting anarchy and dissolution would advance in the world as the twentieth century progressed, ultimately the bloodiest century in human history. And now as the twenty-first gets underway, see if his words still eerily capture our moment: "Things fall apart; the centre cannot hold; / Mere anarchy is loosed upon the world, / The blood-dimmed tide is loosed, and everywhere / The ceremony of innocence is drowned; / The best lack all conviction, while the worst / Are full of passionate intensity." Hope often begins with the naming of truth. I think that's the poet's intent.

In *Alice in Wonderland*, Alice says to the cat, "'Would you tell me, please, which way I ought to go from here?' 'That depends a good deal on where you want to get to,' said the cat. 'I don't much care where,' said Alice. 'Then it doesn't much matter which way you go,' said the cat." When was the last time you thought long and hard about where you were going with your life? I suppose this question may seem a tad abrupt. But experience suggests that sometimes it's in the moments we're caught off guard when we're able to hear a stirringly important query like that as though for the first time. So I'll ask it again: Just where are you headed? What gets you up in the morning and sets your feet one before the other? Is it a great cause or a puny one? A bumper sticker caught my attention some years ago and has stayed with me—"When you aim at nothing, you will hit it every time." Funny how some unsuspecting bit of wisdom can stick with you.

A story from the *National Post* uncovers the latest trend in the "naming-the-baby" follies. Seems the consumerist mind has seeped deeper into our collective unconscious, for now parents are naming their children for favorite or popular products. Consider these new names that number in the hundreds each: Chanel, Armani, and Lexus. How about Timberland, Porsche, and Guinness. Even Chivas Regal, Champagne, Nivea, and Pepsi. Naming-the-baby has always provided for interesting family dynamics, no two families arriving at their decisions in precisely the same way. Hard to tell how deep this product-line trend goes or how long it will last. Once upon a time, religious, family, and ethnic traditions provided inspiration. What do we value? That's the question this tongue-in-cheek story prompts. What we value generally sponsors our inspiration and loyalties. Hey, come to think of it, I wonder if I name my little girl "Lexus" if I could get a discount from the car manufacturer.

Professor Anders Henriksson of Shepherd University in West Virginia has kept track of world history as described in term papers and exams at American and Canadian colleges. The good professor uncovered such facts as these: John F. Kennedy worked closely with the Russians to solve the Canadian Missile Crisis; Ferdinand and Isabella conquered Granola, a part of Spain now known as Mexico; Hitler's instrumentality of terror was the Gespacho; and Gothic cathedrals are supported by flying buttocks. Professor Henriksson is on no crusade against the school system but says that he wants to show that the base of common knowledge isn't as wide as we commonly assume. I, too, have always suspected our common base of knowledge has been less than we had hoped. And consider: our democracy depends upon a well-informed citizenry to make competent decisions. Professor Henriksson may not be targeting our schools, but that doesn't mean we shouldn't. Whether we have children or not, it behooves all of us to support our educational system as perhaps our most foundational shared responsibility. I'd rather laugh about something else.

Teenagers and parents alike overestimate how many teenagers are having sex, according to a poll as reported in the *New York Times*. In general the report concluded that "teens express more cautious attitudes and values toward sex than is perhaps generally believed." A full 85 percent of teens said sex should occur only in a long-term, committed relationship, which is up over preceding years. And contrary to a popular mythology, the majority of teenagers wished their parents were bolder in advising them about decisions concerning sex. "Adults continue to underestimate their influence," the sponsor of the report said. "They may be so concerned about being friends or pseudo-peers that they forget that the primary job of parents is to be parental." It turns out, parents are the single biggest influence on teenagers' decisions about sex, but they don't realize it. Seems to me that's a pretty dangerous disconnect.

IX

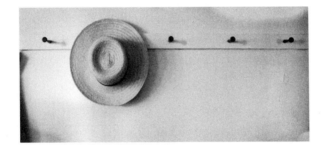

The young man in my office kept repeating the same question: Why should he go into work? It just seemed so meaningless now, so inconsequential. His office had been on an upper floor of the first of the towers to crash into fiery rubble. Though late for work that day, his life, as he had been living it, was completely demolished. He couldn't muster enthusiasm for his prior pursuits. They seemed trivial now. What he really cared about were people. I told him I understood. Among the most affective moments I had on September 11th were my phone calls to my son and daughter away at college. Each conversation ended with, "I love you. I love you too." These simple words spoke with an eloquence on that day that Shakespeare himself could not have written. Evidently this instinct for loving relationship is among the most elemental of human characteristics. Though eventually all would go back to work, it occurred to me to make note of the simple truth that might be forgotten once the state of shock wore off.

Standing in a crowded subway I overheard a conversation between two men. Evidently they were both in the grocery business, the older something of a mentor for the younger. The gray-haired man was sharing how much he liked his work. I surmised he was a buyer, because he allowed how he wasn't crazy about meats, but produce, now that was something he really cared about. He described with deep sincerity how he valued choosing the very best produce he could find. The young man sat leaning forward, taking in every word. Listening, it struck me how much our quality of life depends upon people caring deeply about what they do. And it doesn't matter whether their jobs place them at the head of a corporation, in the middle of a grocery store, or in the driver's seat of a sanitation truck. Taking pride in the quality of one's work is a fundamental building block of civil society. It's worth remembering whenever you see it modeled—the passion of the produce man made me think about my own work a little bit differently.

I was comfortable in bed enjoying a pleasant state of semisleep at four o'clock in the morning, nineteen stories above the city streets, when I became aware of a distant trumpeting. It was a low, resonant bellowing drawing closer in regular intervals. In my sleep state I imagined the calls of a giant herbivore roaming some nearby Jurassic Park, but as the mental fog cleared I realized my dream was prompted by the far more mundane reality of brake drums on a garbage truck making its way down Second Avenue. Fully alert, I found that instead of a typical anger surfacing at having been awakened, I was strangely reassured that those guys were out there doing their job. I got to thinking about the fantastic complexity of the city and how utterly dependent on one another we are for the quality of our shared life. It's good to remember this city—like every village, town, and nation—runs about as well as all of us want it to run. It's about as clean as we want it to be, and it's about as civil as we are.

Beneath a resurgent patriotism and behind the simmering outrage of violation and loss, a profound spiritual truth exposed on 9/11 strains to remain in our conscious awareness. This truth is revealed in the targets themselves: two of the mightiest symbols of power and wealth in the world were brought crashing down to their foundations. In the world's financial capital no amount of money made any difference at all as the towers fell. None. No accomplishment, no fame or notoriety, no amount of preplanned security, no level of striving for comfort, no access to power—none of this made the slightest bit of difference when the towers came down in the wealthiest city in the wealthiest country in the world. The most impressive and powerful works of humanity mattered nothing at all, which, I think, unnerves those of us who thought our power and might had made us mostly invulnerable. The spiritual truth that's available to us is the recognition that our truest strength is, and always has been, located somewhere else.

A *New Yorker* cartoon by Peter Steiner depicts two dogs at a computer. One instructs the other, "On the Internet, nobody knows you're a dog." Alas, even a dog's identity is quickly recognized through his spending patterns tracked by resourceful dot-com entrepreneurs. The bones and flea collars charged on his VISA would give him away. Internet anonymity provides only limited cover. People do certainly masquerade in the chat rooms, no doubt duping any number of others who are susceptible to inflated ideas of *themselves*, but early returns suggest that the Internet is only the newest arena for the human propensity for pretense. That particular character issue has always dogged us; computers only make it slightly more interesting for a while. What really would be a dramatic new development is if some new technology actually helped make us more *honest*, more *authentic* in our communication. The question is, would anyone ever use it?

Contemplating the dawn of a new millennium leads me to wonder how long I might survive into the years that begin with the number two thousand. Will it be, say, 2010 or my personal preference, 2052, which would give me a century-worth of years on this planet? The *Harvard Women's Health Watch* reported the findings of two independent studies on longevity. Duke University Medical Center found that women who attended religious services weekly lived longer than those who went less frequently or not at all. Another report from the California Public Health Foundation also found that women who regularly attended worship services had a lower mortality rate than those who did not. And it went further to say that those regular attenders also had better health practices, more social contacts, and more stable marriages — factors that also bode well for longevity. Now if the same findings hold true for men, I might have a leg up. Thought you'd like to know the inside scoop on this life-prolonging secret as well.

Each year I look forward to hearing about the Nobel Prize winners, especially the winners of the peace prize, particularly those I know little about, but who are making a dramatic impact in their home environments, setting an example for others. Take, for example, Wangari Muta Maathai, winner in 2004 and founder of the Green Belt Movement in Africa that focuses on environmental conservation, community development, and capacity building. I get a vicarious charge from these mental and sometimes moral athletes. Their efforts impress as something beyond the normal, which is why I was slightly disconcerted to read of a study of Nobel winners over the years indicating they may be no brighter or inherently more gifted than their peers. Something else explains their success. Among their traits that colleagues noted was their ability to keep going. That's disconcerting, because it suggests that if we had a little more tenacity for our professed commitments, we, too, might make a bigger difference. What does it take to keep us motivated?

How are you feeling about your body these days? Is it your friend or your enemy? If you stand sideways to a full-length mirror, do you suck in your gut or flex any of the three muscles known as gluteus? Do you work out? Wish you worked out? Or have you given in to whatever current trajectory your body is taking? Is it growing older faster than you wish? Do you think about these things much? Recently I fell down a stairway. In midstep I decided to change directions and the rubber sole of my shoe stuck to the step. I fell hard. Though I didn't do major damage, I became acutely aware that I could have. Just like that. By a simple misstep. You may think I'm being overly dramatic, but nevertheless, this has fastened my thinking on the fragility of existence. The lumpy mixture of organic compounds and water we call flesh and bone is quite vulnerable. Still, this frail structure houses the most precious thing we have—life itself. I'm now paying closer attention to the house for the sake of the home.

S erving on the boards of several educational enterprises as well as being the father of two, I've become aware that educators are discovering an ever-increasing level of learning and emotional dysfunction in children across the socioeconomic spectrum. As of yet, there's no agreement as to the cause. Theologian Douglas John Hall has also noticed this and comments, "Our public at large ... after fifty years of visual conditioning has become habitually and notoriously impatient with any kind of speech that requires sustained attention. It is not accidental that 'Attention Deficit Disorder' is the childhood problem of the age. Most of the children's parents also suffer from this disorder. Middle-class restlessness is rampant ... " As Dr. Hall suggests, it's intriguing to consider if our children are simply manifesting the symptoms of a much larger cultural disease. Consider that my radio messages last exactly one minute on a station that prides itself on the brevity of its news reports. Do we all suffer from ADD?

A videotaped message left in the rubble in Madrid following a devastating series of bombs on commuter trains, proclaimed this explanation: "You love life and we love death." Surely that is propaganda meant to frighten. And it does frighten because it seems to be true. In the attack, 191 were killed, 1,500 injured. No question this brand of Al Qaeda-inspired terrorism chills to the bone. How does one combat those who love death more than life? How does one destroy the destroyer without turning into his enemy? That seems a real challenge in these days, which leads me to observe that never in my lifetime has the immediate need loomed so large for people of faith to dig deep into their spiritual resources. A resurgent and profound spiritual vitality is our greatest defense against the nihilism of fear and death—the greatest defense against becoming what we hate in our enemy. And the greatest ally in turning an enemy into a friend.

In the first weeks and months following 9/11, it was common for New Yorkers to share how the tragic event changed their lives. They were deeply stirred by the courage of the firefighters and police and the outpouring of caring by the entire nation. Many returned to houses of worship. They found themselves reconsidering the direction of their lives and matters of greater value than what had been lately capturing their time and attention. This seemed a positive outcome of the tragedy. But as the years accumulate, I've been wondering about the permanence of this newfound depth. Bruce Eric Kaplan captures the point in a *New Yorker* cartoon. Standing in line, one character says to another, "It's hard, but slowly I'm getting back to hating everyone." There has been a great push to get things "back to normal," both in the city and around the nation, which has been an understandable and generally healthy response, but it would be a great shame if in so doing we chose to forget the lessons about sacrifice, commitment, and genuine human community.

Like many of you, I'm a very busy person. I work hard, put in long hours, and often arrive home late. Though I know it's important to have a habit of rest and restoration, often I don't heed my own best wisdom and lose personal focus. I get wrapped up in thinking my worth is directly related to my usefulness and industry. Not long ago I came across a Taoist story that tells of a carpenter and his apprentice walking through a large forest. When they came across a tall, huge, gnarled, old, beautiful oak tree, the carpenter asked his apprentice, "Do you know why this tree is so tall, so huge, so gnarled, so old, and so beautiful?" The apprentice looked at his master and said, "No . . . Why?" "Well," the carpenter said, "because it is useless. If it had been useful it would have been cut long ago and made into tables and chairs, but because it is useless it could grow so tall and so beautiful that you can sit in its shade and relax." Living in the city, it occurs to me we could use a few more trees.

X

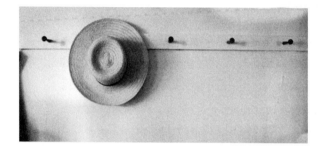

Recently my wife told me I had been sounding whiney and childish. I didn't like her telling me that and told her so, but later realized that I had indeed descended into a narcissistic funk. I had slipped into a mode of thinking that things just weren't going my way and feeling sorry for myself. I picked up an old copy of M. Scott Peck's best-selling book, *The Road Less Traveled*, and read this: "Life is a series of problems. Do we want to moan about them or solve them? ... What makes life difficult is that the process of confronting and solving problems is a painful one." Once before that had struck me as truthful, sober, and obvious wisdom, and it did so again. This prompted a question: was I more of a problem solver or a problem generator? Certainly when I'm whining or carping about this or that I'm far from being a problem solver. And it has become increasingly clear to me that the most effective people I know, whether in their professional or personal lives, are problem solvers. So I've jotted that on a sticky note and stuck it to my computer monitor. My wife can see it there too.

The woman in my office cried quietly as she related her story. She had come because she didn't understand the nature of suffering. She didn't know what to do with it. It seemed so meaningless. Her series of disasters began with the sudden death of her only son at the age of twenty-eight by a freak aneurysm. It continued when her husband was killed in an automobile accident caused by a drunk driver crossing the median. Cancer came next, requiring a radical mastectomy. Anne Morrow Lindbergh wrote, "I do not believe that sheer suffering teaches. If suffering alone taught, all the world would be wise, since everyone suffers. To suffering must be added mourning, understanding, patience, love, openness and the willingness to remain vulnerable." I told my new friend that I didn't have answers the size of her questions, but what I did have was a willingness to walk with her some distance down her path and that maybe together we could learn a thing or two.

Despite filters and blocks, I still receive a fair amount of spam in my e-mail inbox. I know that many of you share my frustration with this. It can lead to the endless search for a spam-free environment — an unending quest in the virtual world for a geographic cure — that mystical place of comfort and privacy, free of external annoyance. It's hard to keep up with e-mail address changes since mail forwarding defeats the purpose of outrunning the spam. But I've become increasingly aware that the box on my desk is not the beginning or end of this problem. Like the kudzu vine blanketing the Southeast, junk information has spread everywhere, into every form of media and every sort of organized human activity. News, sports, religion — even education — are rife with spam that chokes off access to the things that matter most. I'm uncertain what to do about this, but it does occur to me that a cure begins with a diagnosis.

Is it my imagination or is child abuse on the rise? Maybe it's just my awareness that's catching up with the facts, but it does seem that at this moment the news is filled with reports of abuse like never before. The most troubling accounts concern people who are supposed to hold a special trust for children, including parents and other relatives as well as teachers and religious authorities of various stripes. There is no class of people more powerless in our society than children. They cannot speak for themselves; they cannot defend themselves. They cannot organize into protest groups or political action committees. Here's a thought experiment: If children could organize in powerful ways to advance their cause, do you imagine our cultural environment would advance the same values, or that supposed child-centered institutions, like schools, for instance, would remain pretty much as they are? The cause of the helpless is never especially prominent in the world of the self-absorbed. The vulnerable are too easy to dismiss, ignore, set aside—or perhaps better said, abuse.

I recently digitized my television viewing, which means I now have so many channels to surf I'm undone before I turn the set on. The installation also allowed me to go digital with my Internet connection. This new access to the huge universe of information and entertainment is overwhelming. That technology has opened the doors on this immense space, however, has little to do with what one actually finds there. You already know that the websites showing the best bottom-line performance are those dedicated to pornography and television. Well, though I now have upwards of four hundred channels, it's remarkable how little I find worth watching. An old complaint, I know, but today the problem has been compounded to the degree and at the speed of technological advance. During a surfing expedition, a one-minute pass-through on a show entitled *Blind Date* revealed a woman in a hot tub telling a male companion she had never read a book from cover to cover. I imagined, however, that she had high-speed access to four hundred television channels.

In my work I am privy to crucial moments in people's lives. Births, weddings, various life events, and, of course, death. I have always considered this a very, very great privilege. It has kept me close to things that really matter, close to a wide arc of profound human experience. Recently I was speaking with someone whose good friend was in the final stage of an advanced cancer. My acquaintance has been emotionally attentive and caring. A reflective person, she said that her friend's premature end was causing her to think about her own life, and it occurred to her that if she herself were to die today, that she could honestly say she had, in her words, "taken care of business." That is, she had addressed and accomplished much of the personal work that had been presented to her in her lifetime thus far. Not perfectly, she added, but sufficiently. I said that must give her a great sense of peace. She said the awareness came as a little gift in the midst of her grief. Afterwards, I began wondering if I had "taken care of business." In a deafening silence I realized this was a very mature perspective. Given that I consider it a privilege to be able to address you about these important matters, I thought I would pass on her comment.

Are you a moral person? If those reading this small piece reflect the ratios in the national polls at the time, you agreed with the large majority of the American population who reported they were sick unto death of all matters pertaining to the impeachment of President Bill Clinton. I counted myself among that majority, but still found many of the issues demanding of mature, sustained attention: constitutional democracy, virulent partisanship, and public versus private character. But at the center of all this was the moral quagmire swirling around the man who occupied the White House. And here I emphasize the word "man." At the end of the day, Bill Clinton was neither more nor less than that, albeit an exceedingly powerful man for a bit of time. Still, for all that power, I was struck by the human scale of the decisions that got him into his initial predicament. Unchecked decisions accumulating over time are what tripped him up. In other words, at the center of all the brouhaha was a man caught in his humanity, such as it was. And on that point it seemed to me that all of us were included in the conversation ... in our own humanity, such as it was/is. Which begs the question: are you a moral person?

ABuddhist monk attending a gathering of American Vietnam veterans shared this story: During the war, a young Vietnamese woman was killed. She left behind her husband and young son. Needing work, the husband often left the child with neighbors. After one trip he returned to find the village demolished. Searching through the rubble he found some small bones he was certain were those of his young son. He wrapped them up and carried them with him wherever he went. Many years passed when one night he heard a knock on his door. "Who's there?" he called. "It is your son," the voice replied. The old man yelled, "You are a fake and cruel man. My son is dead. Leave me alone." Eventually the pounding stopped. The young man gave up and left. The monk concluded, "The old man never found happiness and lost his son who was still living. Why? Because he was determined to hold on to the bones of the past." Friends, I'll take the gamble and presume to say, "It's time to do some letting go ... "

Roger Swain writes: "Living in the fast lane means being chronically short of both time and breath. When you have to gulp your air, there is no time to savor it, no time to let it linger in the nose. You might as well try to listen to music wearing earmuffs or look at art from behind dark glasses. We live in a world whose odors are as rich and varied as its sights and sounds, but those who rush through it end up smelling nothing beyond their own sweat. To slow down is to discover that, in more ways than one, you smell better." That's good advice. Important advice. I wish I had heard that before my children were born. Well, for that matter, before so many things that have come and gone. Like the days of my own life, for instance. To do what Swain admonishes requires an inner stillness, I think, an inner wisdom that "knows" the secret about life that has absolutely nothing whatsoever to do with most of our pursuits. Why do you suppose we relentlessly settle for secondary ends that cost us so very much? There is so much that smells good, and it starts within us.

When his stroke occurred, Robert McCrum was just forty-two years old and the editor-in-chief of a major publishing house. He had been married just two months when he awoke one morning unable to get out of bed. He writes of his long convalescence in a memoir entitled, *My Year Off*. Here's how he summarizes his learning: "I'd reached a point in my professional life when I could almost literally not see my way forward. So it came as a physical punctuation mark, a reminder from my body to pause and to take stock. What I needed was a season of vulnerability. In the language of psychobabble, I needed to get in touch with myself again, and perhaps—who knows?—only a catastrophic physical breakdown could achieve that." Right in the middle of his life, Robert McCrum had an awakening, "I have learned, in short, that I am not immortal (the fantasy of youth) and yet, strangely, in the process I have been renewed in my understanding of family, and finally, of the *only* thing that really matters: love." Sometimes I'm asked if a personal crisis is the only thing that can open one to a strikingly larger awareness, a fundamental reorientation concerning one's life and direction. How would you answer that question?

For the last month I have been attempting my personal variation of the protein diet. This is the first diet program that has come to my attention that seemed remotely manageable to me. It's simple: avoid bread, pasta, potatoes, and other obvious carbohydrates. Now I like all of those things, but having mustered enough self-discipline to try to shed some pounds, I needed a method that didn't require me to count or weigh or figure. I needed something obvious. Something clear, something that said simply, "Eat this, don't eat that." And lo and behold, it's working. Now, sometimes people come to me saying they would like to have a more meaningful life. They wish there was a method, a discipline that could help them shed negative life-habits and instill healthier ones. Something obvious, something clear. Something that will meaningfully relate them to others and the world around them. And I say, I know just the thing they're looking for. It's called healthy religion.

Among the most persistent complaints I hear from people pertain to change. So many people, so much of the time, rail against change in one form or another. The truth is, I find this rather perplexing because even routine experience should dictate to everyone that life is all about change. Life is never, ever static. It's constantly on the move. I'm a witness every morning I look in the mirror to how my body transmogrifies. Author Susan Howatch writes, "We die and we die and we die in this life, not only physically—within seven years every cell in our body is renewed—but emotionally and spiritually as change seizes us by the scruff of the neck and drags us forward into another life. We are not here simply to exist. We are here in order to become. It is the essence of the creative process; it is in the deepest nature of things." I don't know why we're so resistant to this truth, why we want to lock things down in a frozen permanence. If we could, I think we'd embody something closer to a cadaver in rigor mortis than a living, breathing person moving on to our next iteration.

According to a report filed on ananova.com, researchers at Dartmouth College devised a brain scan that can identify race bias. Using a variation of magnetic resonance imaging, or MRI, it was possible to map brain activity when volunteers were shown photographs of another race. This mapping was followed by tasks designed to test mental resources. The scientists concluded that harboring racial prejudice, even unintentionally, stirred up an inner struggle that exhausted the brain. I can't comment on the brain specifically, but I well know that prejudice of every sort exhausts our culture. Considering these results, it would be intriguing to configure other studies measuring other biases built from things like religion, ethnicity, gender, economic status, and so on. I wonder if the scientists had the guts to test themselves. I wonder how any of us would fare.

The young man in my office had come to talk abut tensions in his life. Especially tensions around decisions. He was conflicted. He felt pretty clear about the sort of material success he was after, but uncertain about everything else. So I asked him what he thought he was committed to. What path did he think he was on? Could he describe it? He warned me that he wasn't going to fall for some sappy religious angle. Sappy or not, I countered that everyone has a religion. Everyone functions from a grand operating principle whether or not they admit it. Mostly that principle can be inferred by the wake they leave as they pass through their lives. The tangible content of our commitments tells the tale for all of us, notwithstanding what we say. I suggested he check out the wake he was currently leaving behind, or if he was brave, ask a couple of others what they saw there. Did he want to hear the evidence of what his wake revealed?

XI

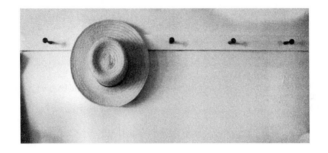

Addressing a crowd during the Civil War, the story goes, Abraham Lincoln was asked why he didn't just declare the slaves to be free and be done with it. Lincoln replied by asking the crowd, "If I told you that a lamb's tail was a leg, how many legs would a lamb have?" "Five," came the answer. "No, four," said Lincoln. "Calling a tail a leg doesn't make it one." This parable came to mind as I pondered proliferating news stories concerning the ethics of our elected officials. It seems simple truths concerning personal decisions and behaviors get swamped under a suffocating mountain of verbiage meant to cover, deflect, and obscure. If ever there was a cause for cynicism for the state of politics, it is this life-threatening allergy for candor and accountability. Calling a lie or a cover-up a truth never changes its essential nature. Smart persons hiding under a blanket of denial can never clear the record. I guess it's time for us common folk to do the modeling for our leaders. Has there ever been a day when it worked the other way around?

Many years ago, while still in graduate school, I heard theologian Henri Nouwen tell the story of a politician, who, in a moment of rare self-awareness, decided to visit a Zen master to ask for wisdom in how he might govern. Nan-in, the Zen master, served him tea. He poured his visitor's cup full and then just kept on pouring. The politician watched the cup overflow until he could no longer restrain himself. "It's overflowing, Nan-in. The cup cannot hold any more." "Like this cup," Nan-in said, "You are full of your own opinions and attitudes. How can I teach you anything unless you first empty your cup?" At the time, I was a cocky young stand-in for the politician. For that matter, I suppose I might as well admit that I've matured into a cocky middle-aged stand-in. The only difference between then and now is that experience has confirmed this basic law of personal physics, which predicts you can't take in something new if you're already full of yourself. Why is emptying so difficult?

In recent elections the issue of character received a lot of play. There were polls galore that monitored the public's analysis of the state of affairs of the affairs of state. Big surprise, the public generally had low regard for the character displayed by politicians. Actually, this simply underscores a growing sense that basic shared human values are withering within our culture. A number of years ago a group of educators and philosophers met in the mountains of Colorado and produced what they called the Aspen Declaration, which listed six core elements of character. They chose trustworthiness, respect, fairness, responsibility, caring, and citizenship. Good list. But I'm mindful that a list has no power in and of itself. Obviously, consensus on how we ought to live is meaningless if no one lives it. Virtue isn't something that can be voted in. It really can't be mandated at all. It must be chosen, one person at a time. Let's not forget that our politics don't exist within a vacuum. They're an organic part of our culture—a sobering thought.

If our recent election is a fair barometer, I would say the general tenor of the electorate reveals only vague interest and involvement. The campaign was passionless. We heard little, if any, soaring oratory to capture the imagination and promote a vision of a dynamic shared future. Very little dreaming or inspiration. Woodrow Wilson is frequently credited as saying, "We grow great by dreams. All big [individuals] are dreamers. They see things in the soft haze of a spring day, or in the red fire on a long winter's evening. Some of us let these great dreams die, but others nourish and protect them; nourish them through bad days until they bring them to the sunshine and light which comes always to those who sincerely hope that their dreams will come true." Seems to me that we are bereft of what Wilson referred to as "big" individuals within our various private and public spheres. I'm not certain why. But it ought to concern us. I wonder how many of us would be considered "big" individuals by those who know us. And what makes someone "big," anyway?

We've been hearing a lot from generals in these last years. Here's a perspective from General Omar Bradley of World War II fame: "The world has achieved brilliance without wisdom, power without conscience. Ours is a world of nuclear giants and ethical infants." Now I don't know if General Bradley had in mind his own nation as well as others, but I'll give him the benefit of the doubt that he did, because every truly wise person I've ever known has their wisdom grounded in humility. They have an ability to understand their own weaknesses and vulnerabilities as well as their strengths. We now say that the United States is the only superpower left on the world stage. Our military and economy have no equal. We know that we are strong. We have bombs and ships and planes galore and an economy that gives us everything our hearts desire. But when it comes to wisdom, conscience, and ethics, what will it take for us to be a superpower?

An article in the *Economist* assures air travelers that mobile phones do not make planes crash: on a typical transatlantic flight, there are a dozen or so left on by mistake. Their use was banned because of possible interference with mobile networks on the ground, although this issue is now being addressed, which will lead to their probable in-flight exploitation. I don't know how I feel about this: glad for the convenience, but wary about the annoyance. I can imagine being stuck in a middle seat between noisy phone addicts who display complete disregard for anyone in close proximity. By the way, there's also no evidence that any phone has ever caused an explosion at gas stations, notwithstanding warning signs, or that they cause cancer. Urban legends all at this point. I thought you'd appreciate an update on this given our penchant to swallow all sorts of popular, though screwy, theories. But while I'm on the subject, how about all of us agreeing to learn when to turn cell phones off? We haven't yet landed on a universally understood and accepted cell phone etiquette—it's overdue, long overdue.

Lest you believe all news is bad news of late and human progress impossible, I thought I'd give you a bit of good news from reliable sources as reported in Toronto's *Globe and Mail*. Since 1990, more than one hundred nations cast aside military dictatorships and chose elected governments. We have three billion more people in the world than in 1960, but global food production has grown faster than the population. Literacy in developing countries has jumped from 47 percent in 1970 to 70 percent today. Global production of ozone-depleting chemicals has dropped more than 80 percent since an international agreement was reached in 1987. And in developing countries a child today will live an average of eight years longer than a child born thirty years ago. Bad news universally grabs the attention of the media—I guess it sells best. We're voyeurs of the dank and depressing. (I sense this pull in myself.) A good antidote: develop the habit of noticing the good while addressing the issues of the day. That ignites hope, which fuels the engine of transformation.

The other day, quite unexpectedly, someone thanked me for something I didn't know I had done. The young man looked vaguely familiar, but I couldn't place his name. He told me we had met on the bus a year and a half ago. David had been in a particularly tough personal place with several very difficult decisions looming. He recounted that with great embarrassment he had started to cry as he told me about his situation. The memory returned to me. I recalled that I had said very little as David spilled out his story. I had simply listened. Nevertheless, he reported that was the critical moment. By the time he stepped from the bus to the curb, he had arrived at his decisions. He was clear. Now eighteen months later David had returned to thank me. I was humbled by the effort he took to track me down. And appreciative. This has prompted a decision of my own. There are some people in my life for whom thanks are overdue. I've never made the effort. I've decided there's no time like the present. Thanks for the reminder, David.

The man in my office said he recently had something of a revelation. It came to him that most people of his acquaintance rarely spoke about a desire to increase in virtue. He knew a few self-righteous prigs, who gave virtue a bad name, but still, he didn't come across many who plainly spoke about their desire to grow in virtue and their difficulty in the pursuit. Complaint about others who lacked it was rampant, but conversation about how to get it or encourage it was strangely absent. I told him I couldn't agree more. This often reproduced quote said to be from the great Native American Geronimo speaks to this: "While living, I want to live well. I know I have to die sometime, but even if the heavens were to fall on me, I want to do what is right. There is one God looking down on us all. We are all children of the one God. God is listening to me. The sun, the darkness, the winds, are listening to what we now say." I told my friend that if he didn't mind, I would share our conversation with some others. He thought that was a good idea.

In 1999, Governor Paul Patton of Kentucky signed an amendment to the state's weapons law that allowed priests, ministers, rabbis, and imams to carry guns in their houses of worship. The original 1996 measure permitting Kentuckians to carry concealed weapons deliberately excluded the clergy, but evidently ministers from rural churches lobbied legislators for the amendment, arguing that if they couldn't carry guns beneath their robes, armed robbers might come after their collection money. Frankly, I've never found the money in the collection plate was so much that it was worth a gunfight. That's because of a basic human condition cleverly explained in the adage: "We all would like to have the reputation for generosity, but we'd like to buy it cheap." Evidently there's a corollary that goes something like this, "We'd all like a reputation for love, but we'd like to claim it with a gun stuck in our robes."

I have a suggestion for you at Thanksgiving. You may think me sentimental, but I suggest that around your Thanksgiving table, with whoever happens to be gathered there, you create an opportunity for each person to say aloud something for which each is profoundly thankful. Shape it like an informal ritual. Allow a little silence between each speaker. After everyone has spoken, see if there isn't a summary prayer or gesture, a toast perhaps, that marks the moment. When my children were small, our family performed this little rite because my wife and I were interested in establishing the practice of gratitude early. I'm not certain whether it was the embarrassment of adolescence or simple laziness, but as years went by we gradually opted instead for a more paternalistic summation that truthfully wasn't nearly as satisfactory. There is something terribly important about our individual ability to express gratitude. Authentic gratitude has direct access to our hearts and our souls. Nothing else so successfully takes us out of ourselves than sincere thanksgiving. We have an opportunity once a year we shouldn't pass up. Of course, we don't have to wait until the fourth Thursday of November. In fact, I recommend any number of dry runs.

S mack in the middle of our most dreadful and
bloodiest war in 1863, President Abraham Lincoln
issued his Thanksgiving Proclamation inviting all
Americans to set aside a day for expressions of
thanksgiving for the many and great blessings that had
been abundantly bestowed even as a terrible scourge
was wasting thousands of lives. This juxtaposition of
disaster and gratitude is compelling. Evidently, crisis
sharpens our focus; blessings formerly ignored are
brought into view, prompting near spontaneous
expressions of thanks. The subsequent yearly
presidential proclamations have become lost in more
recent times, and though families still gather for feasting
and reunion on the fourth Thursday of November, there
is a sense our land is fat with prosperity and lazy with
gratitude. No one would then hope for disaster so that
thanksgiving could abound. Still, it would seem that we
most fortunate of peoples in all the world should be the
most humbly appreciative.

The early nineteenth-century preacher Henry Ward Beecher had this to say about Thanksgiving: "If one should give me a dish of sand, and tell me there were particles of iron in it, I might look for them with my eyes, and search for them with my clumsy fingers, and be unable to detect them; but let me take a magnet and sweep through it and how would it draw to itself the almost invisible particles, by the mere power of attraction! The unthankful heart, like my finger in the sand, discovers no mercies; but let the thankful heart sweep through the day, and as the magnet finds the iron, so it will find in every hour, some heavenly blessings, only the iron in God's sand is gold." You know from your own experience that a person who has gratitude at his or her core is a person who has found serenity. That's because gratitude is the foundational human response to the fact of our existence. When we're grateful, we're in sync with creation and with life. And when we're in sync with life, we move through it with an ability to honor it for the miracle it is.

XII

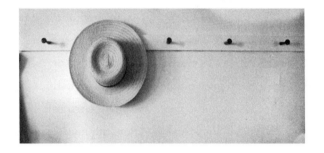

The time between the last week of November and the first week of January is profoundly paradoxical. On the one hand, it frames various religious and civic festivals, which at their best celebrate our deepest sacred values, things like gratitude, humility, compassion, generosity, family, and so on. There's probably more God talk or at least God references during these months than at any other time of year. On the other hand, also during this same time frame, some of our baser values are exploited: greed, commercialism, selfishness, and the like. If economic news and analysis is a fair barometer of shared public values, one has the distinct impression that it is our bound civic duty to spend, spend, spend during the ho, ho, ho season to keep the capitalist engines humming at fever pitch. Now, I'm in favor of a healthy economy, but there's a whole lot more palaver about our spending patterns than, say, our giving patterns, and the truth is, the balance between these competing values reveals the real condition of our soul.

Experience tells me that people tend to fall into one of two camps: those who say "I love you" far too frequently, and those who say it far too little. In either case, there's a dearth of appropriate love among us. And this seems odd, given that, as Victor Hugo said in *Les Misérables*, "The supreme happiness of life is the conviction that we are loved: loved for ourselves — say rather, loved in spite of ourselves." In other words, the knowledge that we are loved and accepted is really the prime need most of us have, which is why there's great irony in our trouble expressing it appropriately to others. My guess is that we secretly don't think we're good enough for the real thing ourselves and we're suspicious about the worthiness of others. So feeling skimped on our fair portion, we skimp in sharing it with others for fear of love's scarcity. Christmas comes round every year to remind us that the more we give love appropriately, the more we will have it. Strange how supremely dense we are. Why can't we learn that it's in the giving that we will receive?

The holiday spirit was drained from me. I had entered a packed Macy's looking for a last-minute gift. I found it half a block later, through a gauntlet they call an aisle. Alas, the salespeople were a hot commodity; short in supply, high in demand. The invisible man, I heard low, guttural sounds forming in my throat as my body began to wobble back and forth. Then, I became aware of someone standing close, speaking to me in low tones. "It's OK, honey," she said. "It's all right. Just be patient. It's all right, honey. Take a deep breath. None of this matters at all. All this stuff doesn't matter." Out of the corner of my eye, I spied a robust woman in an overstuffed coat. "I mean it, honey. None of this has anything to do with the reason for the season. You just stand there and be patient." Tension drained from me, a smile crept up. You say you don't believe in angels? I say they come in all shapes, sizes, and colors for those with the eyes to see and the ears to hear. I left Macy's a renewed man. I found something I actually needed, for a change.

I turned the corner on Fifth Avenue from Fifty-eighth Street when I heard the woman scream, "Donald!" A man several yards in front of me stopped and turned around. The woman yelled, "Don't you dare walk away from me!" and took several long, angry strides to catch up. When she got within range of steaming his glasses, he hissed, "Don't you dare talk to me in that tone of voice!" She screamed back, "I'll talk to you in any tone of voice I want!" and then proceeded to spit the most angry, hateful diatribe I believe I have ever heard. I was momentarily shaken. If looks were actions, Donald would have been on the rack, and she would have been gleefully turning the wheel as his joints popped. It was a nasty exchange. Glancing at their hands I noted both wearing matching wedding bands. They were laden with colorfully wrapped packages from FAO Schwartz toy store, and their holiday exchange was accompanied by a street band bellowing, "Joy to the World." I continued my own holiday gift search more aware than ever that my best gifts weren't going to be found in the store.

One December a number of years ago, in response to the brutal slaying of six International Committee of the Red Cross workers in war-torn Chechnya, Cornelio Sommaruga, then president of the international agency, said this in Geneva, Switzerland: "Every one of us feels deep in his heart the dreadful blow dealt so brutally to the victim's families on the eve of the festive season." It was a "barbarous and cowardly act," he said, committed in the very hospital that the slain workers had set up as "a haven of hope and humanity" in a country devastated by fighting. "Someone wanted to crush that hope." People of good will the world over shared his shock and anger. The horrible event was all the more stunning coming in the season of lights, which in part symbolizes the invincible hope and promise of life that lies behind and beneath our human condition and drives us into the future. It seems every December has its share of barbarous and cowardly acts the world over. War, terror, violence, and privation of every sort form a backdrop to the holy season. There's something about this that underscores why the season is holy in the first place. The season of lights. Light. We are in great need of wondrous light.

Rex Knowles relates in a collection of stories of Christmas that he had shut himself in his study when there was a knock on his door. His children had a play to perform, and he could tell it was a Christmas play because of the lighted flashlight wrapped in swaddling clothes lying in a shoe box. The classic story culminated when his eight-year-old entered, undulating like she was riding a camel, bedecked with all available jewelry. She carried a pillow with three items. After bowing to the holy family she announced, "I am all three wise men. I bring precious gifts: gold, circumstance, and mud." Mr. Knowles says that instead of laughing at this mistake, he prayed. And I have to agree that his daughter's list seems accurate of the things I bring to the altar this year. At any given moment, circumstance and mud might be pretty good descriptors of my experience. But I'm also reminded that the first Christmas story was itself the product of circumstance beyond the control of the characters. It's pretty stunning what can happen to mud when faith, hope, and love have the day.

According to Ross Gittins on theage.com, studies on consumerism reveal that "experiential purchases — those made with the primary intention of acquiring a life experience — make people happier than material purchases. In other words, the good life comes more by doing things than having things." This seems counterintuitive in our shopping culture, considering that money spent on an experience often has nothing tangible to show for it. But this explains in part what I've witnessed in persons who have actually paid for the opportunity to volunteer in areas of need in the city and around the world. What these persons often report is that they have been changed in ways they hadn't anticipated, and never felt better about their lives. Contrast this with research that reveals this fact: the average mood while watching sitcoms on television is mild depression. This might suggest a bit of soul-searching as you trot off to upgrade to hi-definition plasma. After all, it's all about what delivers the most bang for your buck.

Whatever else the holiday season may be for us, one thing we cannot deny: its roots are religious. That's why a whole lot of folks who haven't darkened the door of a house of worship for a year or more may stumble into one sometime during the month of December. This time of year is evocative of neglected sentiments and values. Persons get to feeling nostalgic for missing pieces of their lives. Why they've left the sacred elements behind runs the gamut from simple laziness to remembered wounds of past associations. I read a story once about when the uncle of the writer stopped going to mass, asserting that he did not like the priest. The writer's grandmother responded, "You don't like the bartender either, but you go for a whiskey when you want one!" He concluded that his grandmother was a better theologian than he ever imagined. Here's a suggestion: whatever your particular faith perspective, take the opportunity of the season and practice it.

For a wide variety of religious people, December is the month of lights. Much is made of the lighting of candles and the imagery of light generally, for at the heart of authentic religious practice is the experience of enlightenment, of coming to see the truth that has formerly been hidden. Stories are shared like this one. An old rabbi once asked his pupils how they could tell when the night had ended and the day had begun. "Could it be," asked one of the students, "when you can see an animal in the distance and tell whether it's a sheep or a dog?" "No," answered the rabbi. Another asked, "Is it when you can look at a tree in the distance and tell whether it's a fig tree or a peach tree?" "No," the rabbi answered again. "Then when is it?" the pupils demanded. "It is when you can look on the face of any man or woman and see that it is your sister or brother. Because if you cannot see this, it is still night."

In a *New York Times* article, writer Paul Rudnick mused that "we live in a world where Bed Bath & Beyond sells menorahs molded with characters from the Winnie-the-Pooh books, where images of Jesus miraculously appear on taco shells, and where fans admire Madonna's study of the cabala and its effect on her toned triceps. In groping for spiritual exaltation, I've decided that there is only one god I can worship without question: comedy." In such a world as this, to walk through the doors of a house of worship at this time of year and do the odd sorts of things that are done inside is a rather countercultural activity. At least it is if you go for something other than comedy, accompanied by something other than a sophisticated cynicism that demotes everything to the status of banality. Comedy can make something of the silly, but smart people know the human spirit needs real food. Hungry people know that as well. How to feed the soul—that seems the great dilemma of our day.

A television commercial caught my attention. What brought my gaze from the paper to the flickering screen was the music—a rousing rendition of the last movement of Beethoven's Ninth Symphony whose melody is known as "Ode to Joy," or the hymn, "Joyful, Joyful, We Adore Thee." When I looked up I saw a large group of crash dummies singing exultant praises to a new model of luxury car. And with that, I confess, my heart sank. Not that the ad wasn't clever and well produced. It was all of that. But it struck me as symbolic of our time that crash dummies would be singing praises to a car, utilizing one of the most remarkable achievements of Western music; strangely emblematic of how divested our culture has become of a sense of the sacred in life. In our time, nothing is outside the bounds of exploitation. Everything is fair game if it means making a buck. Everything serves commercial ends. We expect it. Just the way it is, we say. One clever little ad isn't anything to get worked up over, you may think. Get over it, you may say. What's the big deal?

I guessed the young woman who had come to see me one December was in her mid-twenties. She was very pregnant. As she spilled out her story, tears welled in her eyes. She had fallen in love. The young man had spoken of commitment, but when he discovered they had conceived a child, he fled, leaving her very alone. Some combination of instinct and "in-your-face" resolve led her to quickly decide to keep the child. Now, with less than a month to go before delivery, she had fallen into a great depression. She had lost hope. Her job was precarious, and anyway, wasn't our culture hostile to children? Wasn't it an impossible task for a single career woman, with no family to speak of, to raise an emotionally healthy child? Because of the time of year, it came to me to remember the story of another young, single, pregnant woman who conceived and delivered an infant boy in dangerous days. And though difficult, wasn't the gift of life the harbinger of hope? She promised she would think about that.

The new year looms. No matter how one counts the years, no one could dispute we live in momentous times—seemingly never-ending prosperity coupled with political agitation, genetic manipulation, technological innovation, and moral fermentation. In these turbulent days, captured by the cliché, "change is the only constant," we shed traditions faster than clothes on a hot summer day at the beach. Our current generation, though offered an unprecedented life span, has the shortest memory. This month offers opportunity to reconnect with sustaining traditions, but this requires an act of will because these traditions lie submerged under the tidal force of a thousand distractions. More than ever before, we need strong, resilient ties to the source of life and meaning. An oak that aspires to great height must have roots that sink deep. What's the status of your root system?

CREDITS

Henry Ward Beecher in *Life Thoughts Gathered from the Extemporaneous Discourses of Henry Ward Beecher 1858*. Whitefish, Mont.: Kessinger Publishing, 2003.

Omar Bradley in *The Collected Writings of General N. Bradley*. Chicago: University of Chicago Library, n.d.

Orson Scott Card, *Alvin Journeyman*. New York: Tom Doherty Associates, LLC, 1995.

Lewis Carroll, *Alice's Adventures in Wonderland*. 1865.

Douglas Coupland, *Life After God*. New York: Simon and Schuster, Inc., 1994.

Stephen R. Covey, *The Seven Habits of Highly Effective People*. New York: Simon and Schuster, 1989.

Dalai Lama, *Ethics for the New Millenium: His Holiness the Dalai Lama*. New York: Riverhead Books, 1999.

Fyodor Dostoyevsky, *The Insulted and Injured*. Kila, Mont.: Kessinger Publishing, 2004.

Frederick Douglass, "The Claims of the Negro Ethnologically Considered" in *African-American Social and Political Thought 1885-1920*. Edited by Howard Brotz. New Brunswick, N.J.: Transaction Publishers, 1991.

Harry Emerson Fosdick, *The Meaning of Faith*. Nashville: Abingdon Press, repr. 1982.

Ross Gittins, "Why reading is more fun than TV," theage.com, February 18, 2004.

Rumer Godden, *A House with Four Rooms*, New York: William Morrow & Co., 1989.

Douglas John Hall, pers. corres., February 6, 2006.

Mark Harris, "The Game of Life," *Utne Reader,* March/April 2001.

George Harrison in *The Beatles: The Dream Is Over* by Keith Badman. London: Omnibus Press, 2002.

Václav Havel, *Disturbing the Peace*. New York: Vintage, 1991.

Anders Henriksson, *Noncampus Mentis*. New York: Workman, 2002.

Gertrude Himmelfarb, *Liberty and Liberalism*. New York: Knopf, 1974.

Susan Howatch, *Absolute Truths*. New York: Alfred A. Knopf, 1995.

Victor Hugo, *Les Misérables*. 1862.

Carl Jung, "Crazy Times," *New York Times*, November 19, 1993.

Jane Kallir, *Grandma Moses: 25 Masterworks*. New York: Harry N. Abrams, Inc., 1997.

Søren Kierkegaard, *Parables of Kierkegaard*. Edited by Thomas Oden. Princeton, N.J.: Princeton University Press, 1978.

Rex Knowles, "Gold, Circumstance and Mud" in *Treasured Stories of Christmas: A Touching Collection of Stories that Brings Gifts from the Heart and Joy to the Soul*. New York: Inspirational Press, 1997.

Anne Morrow Lindbergh, "Lindbergh Nightmare," *Time,* February 5, 1973.

Scott McCartney, "If the Pitcher Lifts His Pinkie, Odds Are He's a Texas Ranger," *Wall Street Journal,* March 2, 1998.

Robert McCrum, *My Year Off: Recovering Life After a Stroke.* New York: W. W. Norton, 1998.

Mississippi River Beautification and Restoration Project in *Hope Magazine,* July/August 2003.

Parker J. Palmer, *Let Your Life Speak.* San Francisco: Jossey Bass, 2000.

M. Scott Peck, *The Road Less Traveled.* New York: Simon and Schuster, 1978.

Chaim Potok, foreword to *The Holocaust Museum in Washington* by Jeshajahu Weinberg and Rina Elieli. New York: Rizzoli, 1995.

Chaim Potok, *The Chosen.* New York: Simon and Schuster, 1967.

William Rouse, *Best Laid Plans.* New York: Prentice Hall, 1994.

Paul Rudnick, "If Sex Has Lost Its Shock Value, How about God?" *New York Times,* December 6, 1998.

J. D. Salinger, *The Catcher in the Rye.* Boston: Little, Brown and Company, 1945.

Albert Schweitzer, *Out of My Life and Thought: An Autobiography.* New York: Henry Holt and Company, Inc., 1933, 1949.

Aleksandr I. Solzhenitsyn, *The Gulag Archipelago 1918-1956: An Experiment in Literary Investigations.* New York: Harper and Row, 1974-1978.

Roger Swain, *Saving Graces: Sojourns of a Backyard Biologist.* Little, Brown & Co., 1991.

Bishop Desmond Tutu in *Facing the Truth with Bill Moyers,* PBS, March 30, 1999.

Evelyn Underhill, *The Spiritual Life.* Harrisburg, Penn.: Morehouse, 1984.

Volvo Life Award in *Hope Magazine,* July/August 2003.

George Washington in *Wit and Wisdom of the American Presidents: A Book of Quotations.* Edited by Joslyn Pine. Mineola, N.Y.: Dover, 2001.

Jodi Wilgoren, "School Cheating Scandal Tests a Town's Values," *New York Times,* February 14, 2002.

George F. Will, "'Privileging' Postmodernism," *Newsweek,* February 5, 2001.

Edward O. Wilson, pers. corres., January 27, 2006.

David J. Wolpe, *Teaching Your Children About God: A Modern Jewish Approach.* New York: Holt, 1993.